Demons
and
How to Deal with Them

DAG HEWARD-MILLS

Parchment House

1. Excerpt in Chapter 4, from *Five Great Evangelists*, by J. H. Armstrong. Used by permission of Christian Focus Publications.
2. Excerpt in Chapter 23, from S*nakes in the Lobby*, page 13-22, by Scott MacLeod. Copyright Scott MacLeod, Used by permission.
3. Excerpt in Chapter 24, from *The Final Quest*, page 16-19, by Rick Joyner Copyright Rick Joyner, Used by permission.

First published by Parchment House 2005
7th Printing 2014

Find out more about Dag Heward-Mills at:

Healing Jesus Campaign
Write to: evangelist@daghewardmills.org
Website: www.daghewardmills.org
Facebook: Dag Heward-Mills
Twitter: @EvangelistDag

Dedication
To my son the prophet: *Kakra Baiden*
Thank you for your faithfulness and a great work done in Kumasi, Ghana

ISBN: 978-9988-596-02-6

Contents

Chapter 1

The Ultimate Model of Demon Activity

And they came over unto the other side of the sea, into the country of the Gadarenes.

And when he was come out of the ship, immediately there met him out of the tombs a man with an unclean spirit, Who had his dwelling among the tombs; and no man could bind him, no, not with chains: Because that he had been often bound with fetters and chains, and the chains had been plucked asunder by him, and the fetters broken in pieces: neither could any man tame him.

And always, night and day, he was in the mountains, and in the tombs, crying, and cutting himself with stones.

But when he saw Jesus afar off, he ran and worshipped him, And cried with a loud voice, and said, What have I to do with thee, Jesus, thou Son of the most high God? I adjure thee by God, that thou torment me not. For he said unto him, Come out of the man, thou unclean spirit.

And he asked him, What is thy name? And he answered, saying, My name is Legion: for we are many. And he besought him much that he would not send them away out of the country.Now there was there nigh unto the mountains a great herd of swine feeding. And all the devils besought him, saying, Send us into the swine, that we may enter into them.

And forthwith Jesus gave them leave. And the unclean spirits went out, and entered into the swine: and the herd ran violently down a steep place into the sea, (they were about two thousand;) and were choked in the sea. And they that fed the swine fled, and told it in the city, and in

the country. And they went out to see what it was that
was done.

And they come to Jesus, and see him that was possessed
with the devil, and had the legion, sitting, and clothed,
and in his right mind: and they were afraid. And they that
saw it told them how it befell to him that was possessed
with the devil, and also concerning the swine. And they
began to pray him to depart out of their coasts.

And when he was come into the ship, he that had been
possessed with the devil prayed him that he might be with
him. Howbeit Jesus suffered him not, but saith unto him,
Go home to thy friends, and tell them how great things
the Lord hath done for thee, and hath had compassion
on thee.

And he departed, and began to publish in Decapolis how
great things Jesus had done for him: and all men did
marvel.

Mark 5:1-20

The study of the mad man of Gadara is the study of the
pathology of demon activity. You will learn many things
about Satan and demons by just studying this case. Many
people wonder what pathology is all about. We often wonder
why somebody will spend his time studying dead bodies. I did
not understand as a medical student, how important it was for a
doctor to spend time dissecting dead people. I thought, "Once
they are dead, they are dead, just leave them alone!"

However, I came to understand that pathology is the study of
the effect of various diseases on the human body. It is the study
of the ultimate effect of disease. In other words, to understand
what will happen if a disease is allowed to run its course, you
must study pathology. Often, it is only in a dead body, that you
will see the ultimate effect that diseases have.

For instance, if you dissect the dead body of a man who died
from long-standing hypertension, you will notice changes in his
heart, his blood vessels and his kidneys. These changes will help

you to understand what hypertension is currently doing to people living with the disease.

By studying the dead body, which has experienced a full-blown manifestation of a particular disease, doctors understand much more about diseases. Similarly, by studying the mad man of Gadara, you will understand the ultimate effect of demon activity in a human being.

The story of the mad man of Gadara, is a study of the highest kind of demon infiltration. It is a revelation of what Satan would like to do to you if he had the chance. Every feature of the mad man's existence reveals a demonic trait. His condition shows different aspects of Satan's vision for you and I. If Satan had his way, you and I would end up in the same condition.

Even though most people will not become full blown "mad men of Gadara", most of us will experience to a lesser extent the same demonic trends that are demonstrated in this mad man.

The testimony of the mad man of Gadara shows us three things:

1. What demons would like to do to you if they had the chance.

2. What demons are doing to people, albeit in a gradual way.

3. The final state of a person in whom demons have had full expression.

As you read this book, God will reveal many things to you about the activities of demons, and how they affect you.

You will be delivered from demon activity by the time you finish this book.

Many think that the testimony of the mad man of Gadara is the story of a lunatic who belongs to a mental institution. They think to themselves, "Since I am not a mad man, this story does not concern me." On the contrary, this testimony concerns all of us.

Understanding the activities and intentions of your enemy are vital to winning any war. If you want to win the fight against evil spirits, you must know how and where your enemy operates. You must know what the enemy is planning against you.

Lest Satan should get an advantage of us: for we ARE NOT IGNORANT OF HIS DEVICES.

2 Corinthians 2:11

Chapter 2

Darkness – The Home of Demons

...we wrestle...against the rulers of the DARKNESS of this world...

Ephesians 6:12

The darkness of this world is the home of evil spirits. Darkness speaks of the environment in which evil flourishes. Satan rules in the darkness of this world. Deception is a type of spiritual darkness. This is because the environment of deception is the breeding ground for evil spirits.

Darkness is simply the atmosphere of deception under which Satan operates. Our defeated foe flourishes in the deepest darkness. He stands no chance when we come out into the light. This is why Satan hates the Word of God so much.

Jesus is the Light that destroys Satan's influence over men. He is the Word of God. The Word of God is a light that shines in the darkness. Demon activity is greatly reduced where the Word of God is taught.

And THE LIGHT SHINETH IN DARKNESS; and the darkness comprehended it not.

John 1:5

The power of Satan against the church can be likened to several wars and conflicts in the world today. When a super-power fights against an inferior army, the weaker side often knows that he does not stand a chance in open conventional warfare. Therefore, he hides and fights from a position of secrecy, deception and darkness. This often results in guerilla warfare and terrorist activities.

For instance, the army of Israel is far more superior to the armies of the Palestinians; the Palestinians do not stand a chance against the military might of Israel. Israel is even said to be a nuclear power. Because Palestine does not stand a chance, they resort to surprise suicide attacks and terrorist activities. Hijacking planes and killing members of the Olympic squad of the Israelis are just a few examples of the kind of warfare that the weaker army engages in.

Terrorist attacks like the one on September 11 are other examples of a weaker and smaller army fighting against a gigantic force. Similarly, the army of demons arrayed against the church, is no match for the power of God. The weapons of our warfare are mighty.

(For the weapons of our warfare are not carnal, BUT MIGHTY THROUGH GOD to the pulling down of strong holds ;)

2 Corinthians 10:4

Satan trembles at the mention of the name of Jesus. Demons shiver when we sing about the blood. When they see the blood, they pass over. The Word of God is a mighty sword, which slices fallen angels and evil spirits into shreds. In the realm of the spirit, we are a nuclear power fighting against an army of natives brandishing swords.

Because the devil has no chance against us, the mainstay of his operations is through deceptive tricks. The Bible calls these "the wiles of the devil". Our greatest effort therefore must be to uncover the tricks and the traps of our illusive enemy.

Believe it or not, one of the most successful tricks of the enemy is to make people believe that the devil does not exist. This amazing lie is so successful that the devil has used it on multitudes of unsuspecting Europeans. Most European nations are plagued with hordes and hordes of demons. The neat pavements and quaint roads with perfectly arranged buildings will deceive the unspiritual into thinking that all is well. I believe that Europe is the darkest continent on this planet. It contains the most immoral, and godless communities on earth. The devil is very successful in Europe because he has convinced them that he does not exist. Through this powerful deception, Sodom and Gomorrah have been recreated.

The more our eyes are opened spiritually, the more the wiles of the devil will be exposed.

Chapter 3

The Power of Christ Confronts Demon Activity Today

Jesus Christ the same yesterday, and TODAY, and forever.
Hebrews 13:8

Jesus Christ is the same yesterday, today and forever. One of the common things that I have seen under the sun (that is on earth), is what happens when someone meets a friend he has not seen for many years. They smile, they chat, and sometimes have a drink together.

After a while, one usually says to the other, "You know, you haven't changed. Your smile is still the same. Your laughter is the same."

He continues, "You talk about the same things."

He goes on, "You still talk about the Lord. Your passion for soul- winning does not seem to have diminished. You are still preaching on buses and at crusades."

It is indeed not unusual for a man to meet his friend after many years and declare for instance, "You have not changed, and you still eat a lot."

What makes people say to one another, "You haven't changed, you are still the same?"

The answer is simple. When someone does the same things he used to do, it is said that he has not changed; he is the same.

Jesus Christ is the same yesterday and today. What makes Him the same yesterday, today and forever? The answer is simple. He does the same things today that He used to do years ago. Years ago, He healed the sick and cast out devils. Today, He still heals the sick and casts out devils. Years ago, He visited people's homes and blessed them. Today, He still visits our homes and blesses us. He raised the dead two thousand years ago and is still raising the dead in today's world. He is the same. Accept it! Believe it today. Jesus is alive and He is stretching out His hand to minister to you now. He has not changed at all.

He loves to do the things He used to do. That is a hallmark of the ministry of Christ. I have personally seen the Lord Jesus healing the sick and casting out devils today. He has not changed. Do not let the devil deceive you. The things you read in the Bible are real and are still happening today. One of the highest kinds of deceptions is to think that the Bible is just a history book describing the miracles of a Jewish zealot who is not relevant in this modern, computerized society.

There are still mad men like the mad man of Gadara and Jesus still heals such people. There are still many epileptics, who convulse and foam at the mouth. The power of Jesus still heals such people. There are still many, many women with gynaecological problems like the woman with the issue of blood. Jesus still heals such gynaecological diseases. There are many blind people in the world today. There are now schools for the blind. Christ Jesus opens blind eyes today. I have seen blind people receiving their sight in my ministry. There are many lame people in the world. Jesus is still healing such people.

Is it not amazing to note that the problems are still the same? The plagues that confronted humanity two thousand years ago are still the same. In spite of medical advances, these problems do not seem to go away. It is comforting to know that Jesus is still a healing Jesus. As you read this book, you can expect the power of Christ to confront the evil powers of Satan in your life.

How does Jesus heal today? He heals today through His body. He is the head and the church is the Body of Christ. No matter what the good intentions of the head are, He needs the cooperation of the hands to do His works. Your head may decide, "I am going to read this book," but it is your hands that will be used to lift the book up. Without the hands doing their part, the good intentions of the head cannot be realized. That is why the church must have healing and casting out of devils as a principal activity that goes on alongside preaching.

We are the hands and the feet of Jesus today. He is the same yesterday, today and forever. Allow Him into your life right now to heal you, to touch you and to set you free.

Chapter 4

The Commonest Sign of Demon Activity

And always, NIGHT and day, he was IN THE MOUNTAINS, and IN THE TOMBS, crying…

Mark 5:5

The mad man of Gadara was led by demons to roam through lonely mountains and graveyards. This frightening scenario made the poor man cry constantly. You can see from this that demons love to frighten their victims. Fear is a pervading sign of the presence of demons.

In my opinion, the commonest sign of demon activity is fear. The pervading presence of demons is most easily noticed by the presence of fear. Most kinds of fear are of demonic origin! Through fear, Satan is able to keep most people in bondage.

And deliver them who THROUGH FEAR of death were all their lifetime SUBJECT TO BONDAGE.

Hebrews 2:15

Fear is actually a demon. It is not a mood or an attitude!

For God hath not given us THE SPIRIT OF FEAR; but of power, and of love, and of a sound mind.

2 Timothy 1:7

Evil spirits constantly minister fear. That is why Jesus constantly said to people, "Fear not." When demons have their way in your life, you will be afraid. They will minister fear about every conceivable thing to you. The whole human race is subject to diverse fears. Fear of sickness, fear of death, fear of tragedy, fear of witches, fear of the night, fear of divorce and the list goes on. When people are born again, they initially find it difficult to trust in anything good.

There is a fear of the church; there is a fear of pastors; a fear of the ministry and a fear of disappointment. The ability to walk by faith is the ability to walk free of the fears that plague all of us.

The demon, which controlled the mad man of Gadara, took him into a frightening and lonely place that normal human beings would be scared to visit. This is where the devil had taken the man. You can see from this testimony that because the devil was in control, he placed the mad man in a frightening location. As long as the devil was in control, he kept the man in a place of fear.

When demons are in control of your life, you will be afraid of many things. Perhaps the devil is giving you frightening pictures to scare you. That is what he did to the mad man of Gadara. Through fear, Satan keeps many people in bondage. Read it for yourself:

Forasmuch then as the children are partakers of flesh and blood, he also himself likewise took part of the same; that through death he might destroy him that had the power of death, that is, THE DEVIL; And deliver them who THROUGH FEAR of death were all their lifetime subject to BONDAGE.

Hebrews 2:14-15

Once, I remember going for a prayer meeting in the mountains. I was having a meeting with several different pastors. We were all to arrive from different parts of the country, and converge at this particular location.

Somehow, one of the pastors got there before the rest of us. By nightfall, we had still not arrived. As it got darker, this pastor became frightened. He was scared to be alone in the house because it was a lonely house in the mountain. When we eventually got there, we realized that he had left the house. We found him later and he said, "I tell you, I could never stay in this house alone. It is so scary to be here alone." He looked shaken but relieved to see us.

I thought to myself, "The mad man of Gadara was taken by the devil to a lonely mountain to live all by himself." Not only was he in a mountain but amongst the dead. The devil made him actually live in the cemetery. This is Satan's wish for you and me—to take us to the place of greatest fear. He wants us to live in perpetual fear. Almost all Christians harbour one fear or the other. It hounds us, influences us and guides us.

A cemetery is not a nice place to be; even in the daytime. Some years ago, I remember witnessing to my brother-in-law. He did not like me because I had told him that he would go to Hell if he didn't repent. He was very angry with me. Unfortunately for me, I happened to pick a ride with him one night. I thought that he was going to take me all the way to school where I was going, but to my surprise, when we got to the cemetery he dropped me right in front of it at midnight! I tell you, I was not happy at all to be at this cemetery at that time of the night.

This should tell you how wicked Satan and devils are. If the devil had a chance, he would place you in a cemetery and force you to live among the dead. It is comforting to know that the devil cannot just do what he wants with your life. If Satan had complete access to us, we would be turned into mad men dwelling in fear and isolation.

Let me ask you today: What fears are controlling you? If you are full of fear, remember that you are full of demonic influence. I cannot over-emphasize that fear is not just a thought. It is a demon. The presence of any kind of fear is a sign of demonic activity. If you are afraid to marry because of the troubled marriages around, I can understand you. However, the presence of fear is still the work of evil spirits in your life.

The Three Effects of the Demon of Fear

There are three effects of the demon of fear. These are spelt out in 2 Timothy 1:7. The Bible teaches that God has given us the spirit of love, the spirit of power and the spirit of a sound mind to replace the spirit of fear. Therefore, people with the spirit of fear are unable to love. They do not have power and do not have sound minds.

1. A sound mind is taken away by fear.

When you are possessed with fear, you behave abnormally. I remember one day, I went to a harbour with a group of children to visit a ship. Unfortunately, one of the children was so scared of the ships. She screamed and screamed and refused to get out of the car. In the end, we had to leave her in the car with someone attending to her. The child was totally controlled by the fear of ships. In a sense, this child looked abnormal in relation to the other children. The others were happy and excited about the excursion but she was unhappy and paralyzed by fear.

This is what happens to us when we are controlled by fear. Fear makes us become queer and live abnormal lives.

Evil spirits of fear control many women. They are unable to marry because they fear disappointment and the control that comes through marriage. Women who are not controlled by these fears marry easily. Others watch from afar and wonder how anyone could enter into such an arrangement.

I remember a beautiful Christian lady whose parents divorced when she was about twelve years old. It seems that this experience had so traumatized her as a little girl that she could not get married. Several handsome, responsible and spiritual young men wanted to marry this young woman, but repeatedly, she turned them away. She would enter relationships with these brothers only to break up without any substantial reason.

One day, I asked her why she had broken up with a certain handsome man of God. She could not give any concrete reason. When I told her that she was suffering from fear and pride, she got angry with me! From that time, I was not able to speak to her about marriage. The last I heard of her, she was unmarried and approaching her menopause.

It is only fear that makes a young beautiful girl "abnormal" (relative to other ladies). I am not saying it is abnormal not to marry but relative to most of the other girls in her age group, this lady was a little strange.

Fear takes away the soundness of your mind. Fear can turn you into a mad person. Fear can drive you along a queer road and no one will understand your behaviour.

When the Spirit of God is upon you, fear will leave. The frightening things we see around us cannot govern us.

I know of a couple that got married on a Saturday. Unfortunately, the bridegroom died two days after his wedding. I know a lady whose husband died a few months after they got married.

These are terrible experiences we see all around us. If we were to follow these fears, we would be immobilized and unable to function.

There are tragedies of all kinds everywhere. Planes crash and cars have accidents all the time. People die everywhere and under horrible circumstances. It was difficult for me to fly after the September 11 terrorist attack. However, I realized that if I were governed by fear, my ministry would be odd. I would be a man unable to sit on a plane. I would have to travel from West Africa to Europe by car or bicycle. Imagine that!

I have been in frightening car accidents. If I were to follow such fears, I would have to walk everywhere. The Spirit of God gives us a sound mind. The spirit of fear takes away the soundness of our minds. Do not walk in the spirit of fear. Remember that fear is a demon and whoever follows a demon will not prosper. Always remember that fear is a sign of the presence of demons.

2. Powerlessness is produced by fear.

When fear gets a hold of you, you become immobilized and unable to do the things God tells you to do. When I was beginning the ministry, I was afraid that it would not work. Fear takes away strength! "What about if it doesn't work? What about if she dies? What about if he gets cancer? What about if she is barren?"

There are many things to fear. These fears paralyze you and make you unable to do the will of God.

Go in the opposite direction to where fear is leading you. That is how to overcome fear. Do the opposite of your fears. I know that fear is an evil spirit. I must not be controlled by evil spirits!

3. Love is destroyed by fear.

I learnt long ago that someone who fears me does not love me.

There is no fear in love; but PERFECT LOVE CASTETH OUT FEAR: because fear hath torment. He that FEARETH IS NOT MADE PERFECT IN LOVE.
1 John 4:18

Fear destroys love. It manifests itself in suspicion and uncertainty. If my church members are suspicious of me, they do not love me. If they constantly suspect me of evil, they do not love me. Fear destroys love and that is why perfect love casts out fear.

A fearful partner always destroys the "husband and wife" relationship. Fears and insecurities in one partner can lead to a total break down of marriage. Fear leads to suspicion, accusations and counter accusations. The home is turned into a courtroom where the first accused has to constantly defend and explain every move. It is not easy to be in the accused person's box. Fear is not a replacement for love.

Fear often attacks the most beautiful and blessed people. They have everything but happiness. They are scared that they might lose what they have.

This is what happened to Job! He had everything and was a super-blessed person but he was afraid. When tragedy finally struck, he confessed that he had been fearful all along.

For the thing WHICH I GREATLY FEARED is come upon me, and that which I was afraid of is come unto me.
Job 3:25

Dear sister, you cannot make your husband love you when you are governed by insecurity! You are welcoming an evil spirit called fear into your home!

The wife of John Wesley, for instance, was someone who was blessed to have been married to one of the most committed Christian leaders of all time. However, it seemed that a spirit of fear and insecurity obsessed her. She could not stand the fact that John Wesley ministered to other women through letters. At a point, this great founder had to plead with his wife to be a friend, and not to suspect him or asperse (slander) him anymore. Notice from this excerpt, how John Wesley pleaded with his wife not to be suspicious of him.

> But let me be your friend; suspect me no more; asperse me no more; provoke me no more. Do not any longer contend for mastery; for power, money or praise…Attempt no more to abridge me of the liberty that I claim by God and man.

This spirit of fear seeks to gain control and guide the affairs of its victim. Some people's love is so intense that it manifests as fear and self-preservation.

The spirit of fear working through John Wesley's wife tried to guide his ministry and control it. John Wesley again wrote to his wife asking her to allow him to be controlled by God and his conscience. In other words, he was demanding not to be controlled by a spirit of fear but by God.

> *Leave me to be governed by God and my own conscience; then shall I govern you with gentle sway, and shew that I do indeed love you, even as Christ the church.*

The end of this story is that John Wesley's marriage broke down. Love does not break marriages but fear does. Fear is an evil spirit. The presence of fear is the commonest sign of the presence of demons.

Traditionally, fear has not been labelled as a very evil thing. It is seen more as a weakness that some are prone to. Do not be deceived dear friend; fear is one of the highest kinds of demonic attacks anyone can experience. Fear has the power to totally change the course of your life if you allow it.

A few days before I saw the first dead person raised to life in my ministry, a spirit of fear attacked me. This evil spirit tried to direct me away from the crusade I was going to preach at. I would never have seen the grace of God in that dimension if I had followed the spirit of fear. God had to speak to me in a vision to deliver me from this spirit of fear.

May the power of God set you free from every evil spirit of fear!

Chapter 5

Demons Make People Do Unnatural Things

...had his dwelling among the tombs...

Mark 5:3

...and ware no clothes, neither abode in any house, but in the tombs.

Luke 8:27

The demons that controlled the mad man of Gadara made him do unnatural things. It is not natural to live in a graveyard. It is unnatural for an adult to wear no clothes.

The testimony of the mad man of Gadara shows us that when Satan gains ultimate control of a human being, he leads him to do unnatural things.

Things against nature and things against God's design are often demonic in origin. It is not natural for anyone to live in the tombs of dead men. It is even scary to dwell near the dead.

I remember when one of my pastors moved into his new house. I paid him a visit in his new home. After he took me round, I said, "It is a nice house."

"But I have one problem," he interjected.

I asked, "What is the problem?"

He answered, "I share a wall with a cemetery. There are graves just behind my wall and it makes me uneasy."

I understood this brother immediately because I would not like to live by a cemetery.

However, notice that the mad man of Gadara was led to live in the cemetery itself and amongst the graves. This is an example of how Satan gets his victims to live in an unnatural way.

Homosexuality is a good example of an unnatural phenomenon. It is against God's design. God created Adam and Eve (and not Adam and Steve). In spite of the numerous theories put forth by gay activists, we cannot find any of the animals created by the Lord to be homosexual in nature. I have never heard of homosexual dogs, cats, frogs, or horses. The penis was intended to be naturally inserted into the vagina and not into a rectum packed with faeces.

Homosexuality is an unnatural act and is one of the unfortunate outcomes of demonic activity. Of course, we do not condemn homosexuals. They are created by God and Christ died for all of us. Those of us who are not homosexuals may have even worse perversions in our lives, for which we need the grace of God.

Today, there are websites for people who would like to have sex with animals like dogs, snakes, horses etc. There are women who have specially trained dogs they have sex with. These are all unfortunate and unnatural perversions. The origins of this dehumanizing behaviour are demonic.

Is there anything unnatural in your life? Perhaps demons are giving you these unnatural tendencies.

Chapter 6

Madness

...the man, out of whom the devils were departed, sitting at the feet of Jesus, clothed, AND IN HIS RIGHT MIND: and they were afraid.

Luke 8:35

The man of Gadara was a mad man. He lived in a graveyard amongst the tombs. He was completely bonkers! Psychiatrists would have loved to have him as a case study. It was only after Jesus ministered to him that he had his mind normalized.

There are different kinds of psychiatric disorders. The layman often thinks of all mental patients as "mad men". However, several different mental conditions exist. For example, there are anxiety disorders, chronic pain disorders, psychosexual disorders, personality disorders, etc. The more serious ones are mood disorders, which include depression, mania and schizophrenia.

All about Depression

In depression, there is a lowered mood varying from mild sadness to intense feelings of guilt, worthlessness and hopelessness. There is also a loss of interest generally, with reduced involvement in work and recreation. There is difficulty in thinking, including the inability to concentrate and a lack of decisiveness. In depression, there are also apparent physical complaints such as headaches, disrupted, lessened or excessive sleep and a loss of energy. There may be a change in the appetite with a decreased sexual drive. In severe depression, people are often suicidal!

The Highest Kind of Mental Illness

The highest kind of mental illness is what we call schizophrenia. This is a serious illness, which my lecturer in medical school described as "madness". He used to say, "These people are mad." Schizophrenia is the problem that the mad man of Gadara had. Initially, I used to think that everybody in the mental hospital was "mad". However, with time, I understood that there were some patients who were "madder" than others.

The Lord impressed on me to take a second look at the symptoms of these so-called mad men. The two cardinal symptoms are:

1.   Paranoid Delusions (Fears)

2.   Hallucinations (Accusations)

Paranoid Delusions

Delusions are beliefs (or fears) that are held by the individual in spite of contrary evidence. In a person suffering from these delusions, you will notice a pattern of thinking.

Such people are preoccupied with the supposedly threatening behaviour exhibited by other individuals. Paranoid delusions make people afraid of things that do not exist. "Paranoia" means "fear". Paranoid delusions are delusions in which the person is afraid of something.

These people are paralyzed or motivated by terrible fears that seem so real. This form of thought may cause some patients to adopt active counter measures such as locking doors and windows, taking up weapons and becoming enemies of genuine friends.

Accusatory Hallucinations

The other cardinal sign of schizophrenia is auditory hallucinations (accusations). With hallucinations, the individual hears and sees unreal things. These hallucinations (accusations) are often derogatory in nature. In other words, the person hears people accusing him, insulting him and saying derogatory things about him. The accuser of the brethren is at work!

These two sets of symptoms: paranoid delusions (FEAR) and auditory derogatory hallucinations (ACCUSATIONS), mark out schizophrenia (madness) quite clearly. Simply put, fears and accusations are key weapons of the enemy. Have you ever wondered why Satan is called the "accuser of the brethren"? Through the power of fear and accusations, Satan is able to convert normal people into mad men. Satan also eliminates people through these two weapons. For instance, he used the weapons of fear and accusations to eliminate Christ and send Him to the cross.

The reason that I brought this up is for you to see two strong techniques of the devil when he is taking control of someone's life: The techniques of delusions and accusatory hallucinations (fears and accusations)!

When Satan is given a free course, he will totally deceive. He will paralyse with fear. He will accuse, insult and criticize because that is his nature. These two weapons form the basis of the highest kind of demonic activity unleashed against human beings. Fear and accusations are the hallmarks of Satan's presence. This truth is borne out in the life of Jesus Christ.

When Satan Attacked Jesus Christ

Jesus Christ was the subject of the highest kind of satanic onslaught. He suffered directly from the paranoid delusions (fears) of the Pharisees. The Pharisees feared Jesus.

And the scribes and chief priests heard it, and sought how they might destroy him: FOR THEY FEARED HIM, because all the people was astonished at his doctrine.
Mark 11:18

They feared His ministry, His power and His authority. They were moved with fear and deception until they eliminated Him.

He experienced first hand their derogatory and insulting accusations. Jesus was arrested and treated as a thief. He was insulted and accused continually until He stopped breathing on the cross. This is the highest kind of satanic attack that comes against God's messengers. Make sure you are never an agent of paranoid delusions and accusations.

The two well-known titles of Satan are "the father of lies" (John 8:44) and "the accuser of the brethren," (Revelation 12:10). He is described as "that old serpent that deceived the whole world".

It is important for Christians not to imagine the nature and activity of Satan but to believe what the Bible says. **The principal work of Satan is to deceive and to accuse!!!**

Through accusations and criticism, Satan is able to turn the brethren against each other. He is the accuser in the midst of the brethren. He is the accuser in the midst of the church. Through the activities of the accuser, we turn against each other and destroy each other! Accusations produce guilt, confusion, hatred, pressure and erroneous counter measures and counter accusations. Accusations cause distractions and the sidetracking of a powerful army from its true purpose.

Delusions are the highest kind of deceptions. A deception that a person cannot break away from, is a delusion. The church is labouring under a variety of strong delusions. Delusions of what money is not, have led many astray. Delusions of human quest for achievement have led much of the church into deception. Unfortunately, in the world, right is paraded as wrong and wrong as right. Black is called white and white black.

Do not be an agent of accusation! When you accuse and criticize, you are employed by Satan himself. You are being used to divide the church and to bring hatred where there should be love. The greatest attack of the enemy on the church is not from without, but from within.

An erroneous and zealous delusion of self-righteousness is the foundation of all accusations within the church. Remember that it was the Pharisees (zealous and error-filled religious men), who opposed and accused Christ continually. They brought Him to the cross and eliminated the holiest, the dearest and the best! Through the power of accusation, they ended the loveliest gift of God. You have no idea what you may be destroying through your criticism and accusation. You may destroy an entire church through your accusations.

Do not be an agent of delusions. The words of Christ are the words of God. No particular doctrine or teaching can replace Christ Himself. He is the way, the truth, and the life. It is in our interest to return to the words that Jesus spoke. This is the surest way to save ourselves from delusions.

Paranoid delusions (fear) and auditory hallucinations (accusations), are what ultimately cause madness. This is the highest kind of mental affliction of man. It is indeed the highest kind of demonic affliction. Wherever the presence of Satan is, accusations, delusions and fear will abound. The mad man of Gadara who in my opinion is typical of the highest kind of demonic expression, suffered clearly from these two weapons of Satan.

A church filled with accusations and delusions will seem like a mad house. The world looks on in amazement as we fight each other and propagate erroneous doctrines about God.

May we be delivered from this madness. May the Lord set us free from delusions, fears and accusations!

Chapter 7

Satan Is Trying to Kill You

...he was in the mountains... cutting himself with stones.
Mark 5:5

T he legion of demons made the mad man of Gadara cut himself with stones. Eventually, this action would have killed the mad man. This shows that the ultimate goal of Satan within the mad man's life was to kill him. Satan is called a murderer. Satan is the murderer trying to end your life if you give him a chance.

Ye are of your father the devil, and the lusts of your father ye will do. HE WAS A MURDERER FROM THE BEGINNING...
John 8:44

It is important for every believer to understand that Satan is trying to kill him or her. He would like to eliminate you from this earth. However, it is good to know that Satan cannot do whatever he wants to do. The Bible says "give no place to the devil." Unless you give a place to the devil, he cannot operate against you. Satan needs a foothold in order to proceed against you.

The thief cometh not, but ... TO KILL...
John 10:10

I have watched as I saw Satan trying to kill me. He has tried to kill me through airplane crashes. I have been on two different airplanes that almost crashed upon landing. One was at Heathrow Airport in London and the other at the Kotoka International Airport in Accra, Ghana. At the airport in Accra, our plane (KLM) almost collided with a car and our pilot had to take off again to avoid collision. At Heathrow Airport, our plane (KLM) almost collided with another plane on the runway. Quick thinking by the pilot made him take off seconds before touch down, thus avoiding a head-on collision.

In both cases, the Lord spared my life and permitted me to continue His work on earth. In 1997, while driving to the north of Ghana, I was involved in a terrible car accident and I found my car somersaulting off the road and into the bushes. The grace of God preserved my life again. I came out of the car uninjured.

I have also been under attack from the government. There were times I had to be guarded by armed police. I remember one night I was escorted home in a convoy of eight cars. Stress and illness once almost put out my light. Once again, the Lord saved my life.

Every minister must be aware of this reality. You must take steps to prevent the devil from having access to your life. When you stand up for the Lord, you must understand that you are a target of the enemy. The last battle of king Ahab exemplifies this fact. The enemy's instruction was very straightforward, "Fight with neither great nor small, fight only with the king." In other words, leave everyone alone and deal only with the king.

People criticize the leader as he experiences the attacks on behalf of everyone else.

But the king of Syria commanded his thirty and two captains that had rule over his chariots, saying, Fight neither with small nor great, SAVE ONLY WITH THE KING of Israel.

1 Kings 22:31

The king of Israel, who represented the leader of the armies of the Lord, knew that he was the primary target of the enemy.

The Tree in the Golf Course

Sometime ago, I was walking on a golf course and I received instruction from the Lord. I noticed a huge tree that I had passed by many times. As I looked closely at its trunk and branches, I noticed hundreds of scars on the tree. I said to Rev. Sackey, (my senior associate minister), " Have you noticed the scars on this tree? It has been hit by thousands of balls." Again, I received instruction from the Lord, "This tree is not wounded and scarred because it is a bad tree! It is not in the state that it is in because it is evil! It has suffered countless blows and shocks only because of its position in the centre of the fairway."

Many people are targets of satanic troubles because of their positions in the battle. They are good people who love the Lord. But by their positions as pastors and ministers of the Gospel, they experience numerous strikes from the enemy. They are often criticized for their seemingly numerous troubles. After twenty years of ministry, one pastor's wife said to her husband, *"You at all, when will you have peace?"*

Do not be deceived dear friend, many of these battered warriors will be rewarded by the Lord in eternity.

Close the gaps and prevent the enemy from having a foothold in your life.

The Three-Legged Table

Sometimes there are things that you must do to remove the foothold of the devil.

One day, while I was praying to the Lord about various things that were going on in my life and ministry, the Lord gave me a vision. I saw an unusual three-legged table. The Lord said to me, "The devil stands on this three-legged table to launch attacks against you." He said to me, "You have to dismantle this table by removing each of the legs." Then He showed me what each of the three legs was and asked me to remove them one by one. When I did, I noticed how the strong persistent attacks of the enemy were defused.

Sometimes, there are circumstances that Satan is delighted to have and use against you. He launches attack after attack from that position. Remove the favourite launching pads of the enemy from your life and God will grant you victory over Satan's plan to kill you.

Perhaps, many ministers die before their time due to stress, bad diet and a lack of exercise. These things may be Satan's launching pads. Perhaps, introducing some practical measures may stop the attacks.

If Jesus had not intervened, the mad man of Gadara would have perished in the mountains and joined the dead in the tombs.

May you experience a divine intervention in your life!

Chapter 8

Satan Wants to Isolate You

...neither abode in any house, but in the tombs.

Luke 8:27

Isolation is one of the fundamental demonic strategies in existence. The mad man of Gadara was isolated in the mountains and in the tombs. He walked and lived in solitude, having no one to talk to. The demons that possessed him ensured that he was isolated in the tombs.

It is important for Satan to isolate you if he is going to fully implement his plan against your life. The devil is described as a roaring lion, seeking someone to devour.

Be sober, be vigilant; because your adversary the devil, AS A ROARING LION, walketh about, seeking whom he may devour:

1 Peter 5:8

Are You a Lonely Deer?

All you have to do is to watch a wildlife documentary and you will understand how the devil operates. All the lion wishes for is to get an isolated antelope or a lonely deer. Even as a pastor, I have learnt not to live in isolation.

The Bible teaches that WE have the mind of Christ. The mind of Christ is not with one particular pastor or group of pastors. All of us together have the mind of Christ. That is why we need each other.

For who hath known the mind of the Lord, that he may instruct him? But WE have the mind of Christ.

1 Corinthians 2:16

Anyone who isolates himself is opening himself up to deceptions and delusions. The highest kind of deception is to think that you do not need anyone. We need one another and Satan knows that. That is why he tries to keep us from each other. My greatest advances in the ministry have come as a result of coming near different ministers. Interaction with all of God's children has only been a blessing to me.

Unfortunately, fighting, bitterness and pride have fragmented the church into several isolated segments. The American church rarely learns from the Nigerian church. And the Nigerian church rarely learns from the church in Malawi. The white church rarely learns from the black church. And the Asian church is mostly cut off from the South American church.

As I have travelled to different continents, I have received many blessings from the different sections of the Church. Have you noticed that the first step to backsliding of church members is staying away from fellowship?

I have watched as ministers struggled in their lonely corners. I knew that if they were only to relate with the rest of us, their lives and ministries would be changed dramatically. Isolation is a primary demonic strategy that the church must fight.

May the Lord unite us into one Body!

Chapter 9

Demons Help People to Destroy Themselves

...cutting himself with stones.

Mark 5:5

The mad man of Gadara, fully under the influence of Satan, cut himself with stones. He systematically destroyed himself with stones. This is a very important manifestation of the presence of Satan: self-destruction. There are many satanic and demonic diseases that are self-destructive. Diseases like asthma are overreactions of the body to foreign bodies, which result in self-destruction. The body kills itself slowly as it tries to protect itself from these foreign bodies.

Unforgiveness is one such demonic foothold. Many do not understand that bitterness is self-destructive. By keeping the hurts and the pain, many people destroy themselves. Demons encourage us to bear grudges and to avenge all who hurt us. God will forgive every sin we commit but He will not forgive us when we do not forgive others. Many are not aware that by maintaining a grudge, we are slowly destroying our own selves. There is nothing more self-destructive than bitterness and hurts. I have watched many self-destruct as they kept grudges and hurts.

The great empires of this world have rarely been destroyed from outside. The collapse always came from within. Bitter wrangling, inner fighting and political divisions were always behind the collapse of these great empires of the world. The story of the fifth column is well known.

There was an army general who surrounded a large city with the aim of conquering it. This city was heavily fortified with a high and imposing wall and gate. The army general surrounded the city in readiness to attack.

One friend of the general came along and asked him, "Sir, how are you going to overcome the defences of this city? No one in recent history has been able to conquer this great city."

The army general smiled and said, "It's my 5th column. I'm depending on them to do the trick." The general's friend was very interested and asked, "What is this 5th column? I thought you only had four columns."

The army general replied, "I do have a 5th column."

"Oh, I see. Is it a special commando unit or are they airborne paratroopers?", the man asked. The general laughed, "No, it's none of these. My fifth column consists of my spies, agents, friends and supporters who are already within the city. You just wait. They will open those big gates from within and my armies will rush in."

Destroying the Church from Within

The church cannot be destroyed by an outside force. It will only be destroyed from within. Many people think they are helping God as they accuse fathers and senior ministers of various crimes. They feel they are bringing to order the backslidden and deviant men of God. The accuser of the brethren urges them on and they are anointed from Hell to destroy the church. They generate much confusion and division within the church thinking they are doing the work of God.

> **They shall put you out of the synagogues: yea, the time cometh, that whosoever killeth you will think that he doeth God service.**
>
> **John 16:2**

> **Now I beseech you, brethren, mark them which cause divisions and offences contrary to the doctrine which ye have learned; and avoid them.**
>
> **Romans 16:17**

Self-destruction is one of the key strategies of demonic attacks. When the spirit of Satan takes hold of a person, he will often begin to cut himself with stones.

The prodigal son is a typical story of someone with a self-destructive spirit. He had everything going for him and he dwelt safely in his father's house. By one decision, he destroyed himself and his future. No external force contributed to his demise. It was all self-inflicted; he virtually cut himself with stones.

God raises up fathers and gives them sons. Sometimes the spirit of Satan possesses the sons and they go very far from their fathers. When all is said and done, the prodigal sons are all but destroyed. This is an evil that I have seen under the sun and it is common among pastors.

May God save us from the spirit that makes us put a knife to our own throats!

Chapter 10

Demon Activity Gives Rise to Uncontrollable People

...and no man could bind him...

Mark 5:3

T he fact that no one could bind the mad man of Gadara demonstrates that he had become uncontrollable. No one could bind or restrict him. This is a feature of satanic influence: uncontrollability!

The prodigal son was uncontrollable. No one could advise him. He destroyed himself and his future ministry by moving out of his father's care. There are two types of wisdom. The wisdom from above is characterized by one wonderful feature: It is easy to be entreated.

But the wisdom that is from above is first pure, then peaceable, gentle, and EASY TO BE INTREATED, full of mercy and good fruits, without partiality, and without hypocrisy.

James 3:17

Pride, the spirit of Satan, will teach you to be unyielding and adamant. Humility and the spirit of Christ will teach you to flow and to listen to advice.

Staying under Authority

The mad man of Gadara was not under any authority. No one in the city could control him. God, however, has not designed our lives that way. We are designed to be under authority. Satan is the ultimate rebel who broke away from God's authority. Up until today, he inspires millions to break away from any kind of authority.

The spirit of Satan re-describes authority figures as dictators or tyrants. This is in order to legitimize a break away from authority. Please get this message right: The mad man of Gadara symbolizes the highest expression of Satanism in a man. Ultimately, demon activity will make you rebellious!

The Scripture clearly states that God sets up authorities.

Every person is to be in subjection to the governing authorities. For there is no authority except from God, and those which exist are established by God.
Romans 13:1 (New American Standard Version)

Demonic activity is often directed against three God-given authorities. Since the devil is against God, he is also against the authorities that God sets up. Satanic rebels are against God's authority in the church, which is the pastor. Demonic activity is also against the authority in the home, which is the husband.

Finally, there is demon activity against the authority of the nation, which is the government. God established all these authorities. No one is wiser than God and we must accept His Word. Like the serpent in the garden, Satan will always challenge the wisdom of God's Word.

People inspired by the evil spirit of pride always challenge the legitimacy of the husband's authority in the home. Often, when a wife is influenced by demons, she will reject her husband's authority. Mostly, before people marry, the word of the husband is very important and seen as something to be obeyed and followed. However, as time progresses and demons infiltrate, the words of the husband are despised and rejected. There is an angry reply to every instruction. There is a rejoinder to every bit of advice. I have watched as certain wives became more and more deceived through familiarity. They think they can no longer be deceived and pushed around by their husbands. Often, the reality is that demons of rebellion are at work.

The same thing happens in churches. Deceived church members rise against God's servant, calling him a tyrant and a dictator but they do not know that they are totally deceived. They call for democracy and claim they will no longer tolerate nonsense. Often evil spirits of deception have taken hold of them. One of the highest kinds of deception in the church is to fight against the pastor. Jesus said, "Judge not."

While on earth, we will never see clearly enough to judge correctly. Churches are full of critical and faultfinding people. This is one of the highest kinds of demonic infiltration in the church. Show me a church filled with critical people and I will show you a church filled with demons.

The mad man of Gadara could not be controlled by anyone. In the same way, pastors, husbands or any authority figure cannot control people under demonic control. Authorities within the nation must be honoured and respected.

Every person is to be in subjection to the governing authorities.
Romans 13:1 (New American Standard Version)

When Paul wrote his letter to the Romans, Nero, one of the most evil emperors of Rome, governed Rome. Nero was known to offer up Christians to be chewed up by lions. There were times he set Christians ablaze as torches in his garden to lighten up his parties! Yet, Paul said to the Romans that God establishes every authority that exists. In other words, God established Nero.

Commonly, the people who are opposed to authority in a nation are the criminals and the dark side of society. It is in the rebellious underworld of cities that Satanic and demonic activities thrive. Prostitutes, armed robbers, thieves and criminals are just a few examples of those who stand against authority in any nation.

None could bind him, no not with chains! Is that the description of your life? None can lay hands on you? None can be a father to you? None can be a pastor to you? *None can be a husband to you? None can bind you, not even with chains!*

Chapter 11

Depression and Sadness Are the Result of Demon Activity

...he was ... in the tombs, crying ...

Mark 5:5

Notice that the mad man of Gadara was constantly crying. He was sad, depressed and emotionally distraught. This unfortunate state was caused by the legion of demons in him. It is time for you to believe that a lot of the sorrow we experience is actually caused by evil spirits. If Satan had his way, you would cry everyday!

When Satan has his way in your life, sadness is what follows. Unexplained depression is most certainly the work of evil spirits. It is no surprise that anti-depressant medicines are some of the most used drugs in the world today. The greatest problems of humankind today are not bacteria or viruses but swarms of evil spirits, which invade the hearts and minds of men. It is no wonder that unexplained sadness and sleeplessness afflicts millions.

The mad man of Gadara was a man of tears and sorrows. He was in pain. He was crying constantly. This is the picture of the highest kind of demonic affliction. God is not the author of your sorrows. He is the giver of joy. God is not the one who made the mad man cry. It was a legion of demons, which made him cry. Perhaps, a legion of demons has afflicted your soul.

Receive your deliverance as you read this book! May you fall into deep sleep and experience freedom from demonic attacks!

Contrary to what many think, sadness and depression are not just bad feelings. Depression is not just a bad mood. The Bible calls it the spirit of heaviness.

To appoint unto them that mourn in Zion, to give unto them beauty for ashes, the oil of joy for mourning, the garment of praise for THE SPIRIT OF HEAVINESS; that

they might be called trees of righteousness, the planting of the LORD, that he might be glorified.

Isaiah 61:3

What makes people so sad that they give up on life and become suicidal? It can only be demons.

I remember a medical doctor who went to England to further his education. For no known reason, he was unable to get into the pro-gramme that he wanted to pursue. This man sunk into depression. His friends with whom he lived in London called his parents to inform them that their son was on a plane heading back home and that they thought that their son was suffering from depression.

On his arrival in Ghana, many different people, including his pastor, persuaded this man not to kill himself. However, one fine afternoon, he checked himself into a hotel room, wrote an apology note to the hotel manager, a letter to his parents saying how much he hated himself, and then committed suicide.

This was a bright young man with a promising future. The doctor who did his post mortem examination had lectured him in the medical school and remembered what a good student he had been. Why would a medical doctor with such a bright future decide to take his own life?

These things can only be explained by the activity of evil spirits. What is the explanation to the hopelessness that grips the heart of a man with an apparently bright future? It is time for us to know the source of the problem and tackle it at its root.

Do not forget that it was the legion of demons that made the mad man cry. Perhaps evil spirits are making you depressed and sorrowful. Receive your deliverance today in the name of Jesus!

Chapter 12

Demons Work to Disgrace You!

...and ware no clothes, neither abode in any house...
Luke 8:27

It was the legion of demons that made the mad man walk around naked. Walking around naked in public is one of the highest forms of disgrace.

There are two types of demonic plans. There are short-term plans and long-term plans. It is important for every believer to get a revelation of the long-term plan of the enemy against your life and ministry. Recently, the Lord led me to pray about the things Satan was planning against me. You may not know it, but the enemy is planning and taking decisions about you.

Look around carefully and you will see many who were once financially blessed but are now broke. I know people who once had millions of dollars but today have little or no money. The spirit of disgrace is working against prosperous Christians to bring them to naught. If you are a businessman, it is important to pray about the wealth and establishment that God has given to you.

Many ministers were once men of renown. Today, many of these have been silenced and disgraced. This is the work of demons.

Many tele-evangelists of America have been disgraced and set aside. A closer look at the American experience will reveal that there was a long-term hidden agenda behind the attacks on God's servants.

Psychics have now replaced these evangelists. It was the long-term agenda of the devil to replace God's servants with fortunetellers and soothsayers. The spirit of disgrace was actually the spirit of Satan fighting the servants of God.

Chapter 13

Demons Work in Groups and Teams

...Legion: for we are many.

Mark 5:9

As you can see, a band of demons afflicted the mad man of Gadara. The word "legion" means, "a band, a crowd, a host or a multitude". The mad man's condition was not caused by a single demon but by a team of evil spirits working together. The word "legion", is very revealing as it aptly describes the group nature of demonic activities. Teams of evil spirits carry out most of Satan's plans. That is why the demons answered,"...legion, for we are many."

Ten Common Demonic Teams

Rarely do you find demons working in isolation. There is often a complicated network of evil spirits involved in any evil situation. When there is confusion in the church, you can hardly put your finger on a single cause: Is it jealousy? Is it hatred? Is it disloyalty? Is it carnality?

1. The marriage spoiling team

Counselling with couples often reveals a complex array of insolvable problems. No one even knows the beginning or end of the problems. It may have begun as selfishness, continued as rudeness, anger and pride. Offences pile up and lead to bitterness and unforgiveness. The unforgiveness leads to revenge, unfaithfulness, adultery, hatred, fighting, murder and divorce. As you can see, the problems do not come in isolation. They come in groups. They come as an intricate cocktail of demonic activity.

It is important to know about some of the teams of demons that commonly work together. When you understand this principle, you will know what to expect and how to deal with the enemy.

...and taketh with himself seven other spirits more wicked than himself...

Matthew 12:45

2. The stealing team

The spirit of lying and stealing often go together. Thieves usually tell lies because they need to cover up their activities. Spirits of envy, hatred and murder often work together. The Bible teaches that Jesus Christ was crucified because of envy.

For he knew that the chief priests had delivered him FOR ENVY.

Mark 15:10

3. The future spoiling team

When a young man or woman who is full of life destroys himself through lust, drunkenness, gambling and drugs, the spirits of poverty, criminal activity and prostitution find their way into these people. This is why it is difficult to extract drug users and prostitutes from their complex array of problems.

4. The sex team

When a young person is deeply involved with multiple sexual partners, hosts of demons often flood the person. The book of Revelation declares that Babylon had become the habitation of devils because of her multiple fornications.

And he cried mightily with a strong voice, saying, Babylon the great is fallen, is fallen, and IS BECOME THE HABITATION OF DEVILS, and the hold of every foul spirit, and a cage of every unclean and hateful bird. FOR (BECAUSE) ALL NATIONS HAVE DRUNK OF THE WINE OF THE WRATH OF HER FORNICATION, and the kings of the earth have committed fornication

**with her, and the merchants of the earth are waxed rich
through the abundance of her delicacies.**

Revelation 18:2-3

The spirits of disobedience and rebellion take root. Spirits
of licentiousness, abortion and barrenness follow these. Other
common members of the sex team are the spirits of HIV Aids,
which work closely with the spirit of death.

5. The divorce team

Spirits of deception and divorce often move together. Most
people who divorce are deceived into thinking that there is
someone better than their spouse out there. This is the commonest
deception in the hearts of many couples. This is why a large
percentage of people who divorce remarry the same person.

6. The nation spoiling team

The problems of any country can rarely be diagnosed as
emanating from a single cause. Are the problems due to a spirit
of corruption, bad leadership, deception or discrimination? The
spirits of poverty, sickness and death often flow together. In
countries where there is a lot of poverty, there is a lot of sickness
and a high mortality rate.

An example of demonic teamwork is found in the book of
Revelation:

**And I saw, and behold A WHITE HORSE: and he that sat
on him had a bow; and a crown was given unto him: and
he went forth conquering, and to conquer. And when he
had opened the second seal, I heard the second beast say,
Come and see.**

**And there went out another HORSE THAT WAS RED:
and power was given to him that sat thereon to take peace
from the earth, and that they should kill one another: and
there was given unto him a great sword.**

And when he had opened the third seal, I heard the third beast say, Come and see. And I beheld, and lo a BLACK HORSE; and he that sat on him had a pair of balances in his hand.

And I heard a voice in the midst of the four beasts say, A measure of wheat for a penny, and three measures of barley for a penny; and see thou hurt not the oil and the wine.

And I looked, and behold a PALE HORSE: and his name that sat on him was Death, and Hell followed with him. And power was given unto them over the fourth part of the earth, to kill with sword, and with hunger, and with death, and with the beasts of the earth.

Revelation 6:2-6, 8

In this vision, four spiritual horses with four spiritual riders were seen. First, there was a white horse, then a red horse, then a black horse and finally a pale horse. Each of these horses had a different rider. The first to be introduced was the spirit of a conqueror. The second spirit was the spirit that takes peace away. And the third spirit was the spirit of famine in which three measures of barley were sold for a penny. The fourth was the spirit of death.

One after another, these four spirits ravaged the earth until a quarter of the earth was killed with the sword and with hunger. You do not have to be very old to have seen this pattern. Let me give you a few examples:

Liberia 1990

Some years ago, Charles Taylor in Liberia, came forth conquering and to conquer. His aim was to remove President Doe from power. There was great excitement, as he seemed to be the liberator of Liberia.

Then came forth the second rider whose power was to take away peace. It is interesting to note that peace has never returned to Liberia since this man began his conquest.

For the last ten years, there has been no electricity in that country. Various rebel groups have ravaged the countryside, taking away the peace. Famine set in. That is the third rider at work. As you watch television, you will see humanitarian groups airlifting tons and tons of food aid.

Finally, the spirit of death engulfs the region and we hear of mass graves and thousands of people losing their lives. Demons truly do work in groups.

Congo 1997

In The Congo, we had a similar situation. The late Kabila came forth conquering and to conquer. He marched on Kinshasa to overthrow President Mobutu. No sooner had he accomplished this feat than we heard of various rebel factions fighting within the country. It was now the turn of the second rider to take away peace. The republic became the cradle of one of the largest civil wars of Africa.

Several countries participated in this conflict and peace was taken away from the earth. We all watched CNN as the humanitarian groups airlifted tons and tons of food to dying refugees. This was the third team rider at work. The pattern is frighteningly similar. Finally, the mass graves and the death toll were announced. Indeed, all the four riders had effectively worked together again.

7. The church spoiling team

In the church, the spirits of slander, backbiting, criticism, pride, self-righteousness, judgemental attitudes, disloyalty and church splits collaborate closely. They encircle churches and invade from different angles. Soon the church is embroiled in one conflict or another. It is no wonder that many churches cannot grow.

Jesus taught that when an evil spirit is cast out, he recruits a larger team. A seven-member team of demons will succeed where only one failed.

Then goeth he, and taketh with himself SEVEN OTHER SPIRITS more wicked than himself, and they enter and dwell there: and the last state of that man is worse than the first. Even so shall it be also unto this wicked generation.

Matthew 12:45

8. The depression team

Spirits of broken-heartedness, disappointments, depression, suicide and death also team up quite often. This is why Paul advised the Corinthians not to be too sorrowful. He explained that the sorrow of the world leads to death. The spirits of sorrow, despair and death often work together. The mad man of Gadara shows us the ultimate desire of demons: to inhabit human beings in large groups.

9. The quarrelling team

A quarrelsome person is usually also proud, stubborn, cantankerous, divorce-prone and deceived. All these make up an effective team of evil spirits that work to destroy an individual.

10. The insecurity team

The spirits of insecurity, fear, accusations, selfishness, self-preservation and hatred also work well together. Like partners in an effective team, they often compliment each other. May your eyes be opened to see the group of evil spirits that is unleashed against your life and ministry!

It is important for every minister to have a revelation of the group of evil spirits that are working against him. Some of the problems of ministry are complicated and have several dimensions to them. Without a revelation of what is fighting you, you will find it hard to win your spiritual battle. The Bible calls Satan the "father of lies" and that "old serpent which deceiveth the whole world" (John 8:44; Revelation 12:9).

Chapter 14

Demons Are Territorial

...he besought him much that he would NOT SEND THEM AWAY OUT OF THE COUNTRY.

Mark 5:10

This very unusual request of the demons puzzled me for many years. Why did they say, "Don't send us out of this country?" The demons could have requested a little more time to stay in the mad man. They could have asked not to be cast out in the first place. However, what seemed to concern them was their need to stay in that same country.

This teaches us an important lesson: Demons inhabit particular countries and do not want to move away. These particular demons lived in the country of the Gadarenes and wanted to stay there.

One class of demons described in Ephesians is "principalities". Principalities denote an evil influence that reigns over a territory. It is not difficult to see the influence of different kinds of spirits in different areas in the world.

For we wrestle not against flesh and blood, but against PRINCIPALITIES, against powers, against the rulers of the darkness of this world, against spiritual wickedness in high places.

Ephesians 6:12

In Matthew 12, the demons that were cast out declared, "I will return to my house." Unfortunately, demons have made certain places their homes. None of us would like to be dislodged from our usual habitat. Demons have usual habitats too.

There are spirits of poverty, which occupy certain parts of the world.

You can see the dirty and impoverished roads and houses in areas where these evil spirits occupy. There is often no logical reason why these nations should be the way they are.

The only explanation must be evil spirits.

The spirit of war rests over certain parts of the world. The beginnings of the First World War, the Second World War and the Serbian war, (which have been three of the largest conflicts to hit the world), had something to do with the Serbian region.

In Matthew 12:43, demons are described as needing resting places. Demons are also shown to walk through dry places. Evil spirits need places where they are comfortable. A dry place speaks of a hostile and unwelcoming environment in which no rest can be found. These are places where demons have no rest.

I believe that Satan does not live in Africa but in Europe. Most Africans believe in God. Today in Europe, it is the Africans who fill the churches. I believe that Satan has his seat (his place of greatest victory and relaxation) in Europe. It is in Europe that deception is strongest.

Most indigenous Europeans do not believe in God, in Christ or even in the existence of the devil. How comforting that must be for Satan! Europe is a place where he can call home. Your home is where you lay down to rest. Your home is where you sit down to relax and feel safe. Do you think that Satan feels safe in Africa when meetings are organized to bind him in almost every neighbourhood? Do you think the devil can relax when people are so conscious that he is around? When songs are composed and chanted against you by thousands of people, you will not feel happy. Satan feels threatened in Africa.

Read the words of a typical song sung in African churches,

In the Word of God, there is power!
In the Name of Jesus, every knee shall bow!

As you know, the devil is not omnipresent. He is in one place at a time. In Bible times, John identified the home and seat of the devil. He wrote a letter that revealed that Satan's home was in a city called Pergamos.

And to the angel of the church in Pergamos write; These things saith he which hath the sharp sword with

**two edges; I know thy works, and where thou dwellest,
even WHERE SATAN'S SEAT IS: and thou holdest fast
my name, and hast not denied my faith, even in those days
wherein Antipas was my faithful martyr, who was slain
among you, WHERE SATAN DWELLETH.**

Revelation 2:12,13

As you can see, this Scripture tells us that Satan both lived and sat (was at ease) in Pergamos. I believe that Satan's seat today is in Europe. I do not believe Satan is happy or at ease in Africa. There are too many all-night prayer meetings all over Africa. There are too many open-air crusades going on there. There are too many groups worshipping and singing about the blood of Jesus for Satan to sit at ease there.

One day, I was playing golf in Ghana when I heard people praying and shouting just outside the course. I said to my partner, "Satan cannot live in Africa! Which golf course in Europe has a group of prayer warriors shouting and praying from the bottom of their hearts on a Monday morning?"

At another time in the night I was coming home from a meeting and I put on the radio. It was midnight and there were two young men praying on the air. They were having an all-night prayer meeting in the studio. They spoke mostly in tongues and shouted their prayers to God from the bottom of their hearts. One groaned like a bear whilst the other roared like a lion throughout the night. I thought to myself, "The prince of the power of the air will not like this at all." I said to my wife, "Satan can never live in Ghana!" I knew that a programme like this could never be aired in Europe.

In the letter to the church in Pergamos we learned that Satan had his seat there. This teaches us that Satan was actually headquartered in Pergamos. There are cities that are known for immorality. If you end up in any of these places, watch out because the spirit of the city will be gunning for you.

In Ghana for instance, there are certain harbour cities, which are well known for their immorality. Nigeria is well known to have spirits of corruption, assassination and armed robbery.

There are certain regions in Ghana that are known for their quarrelling and cantankerous nature. Evil spirits of offence drive people in these areas to quarrel all the way into their graves without ever letting up. Other sections are known for witchcraft and voodoo. Some parts of the country are known for their violence and murderous tendencies. These are works of evil spirits, which have lived in these areas for many years.

There are even sections of the road, which are inhabited by evil spirits. Spirits of accident and tragedy inhabit trees along the road. Many mysterious and inexplicable accidents have occurred at these spots. These are the works of evil spirits that dwell in certain geographical locations.

When you come into a new house, you must always sanctify it. Evil spirits dwell in various locations. For instance, a spirit of divorce may have been dwelling in a house that you have just moved into. Inexplicable quarrels may begin to occur in your marriage after you move into that apartment.

I have known of people who had happy marriages until they moved to certain countries. Thereafter their marriages deteriorated rapidly. I said to a divorcee friend, "Perhaps you wouldn't have divorced if you hadn't come to this country." He said to me, "I agree with you 100%; this would never have happened if I had stayed in my home country." He continued. "In my country divorce is unusual but here, even pastors divorce easily."

Whenever I enter a hotel room, I pray and sanctify it before I settle in. Sometimes I lay hands on the bed and cast evil spirits out of the ceiling. No one knows what has gone on in that room before I came there. When you move into a new physical location, it is your spiritual duty to assess what kind of spiritual presence pertains.

Principalities love to dominate areas with their evil presence.

Chapter 15

Demon Activity Exists Side by Side with Worshipping Christians

...when he saw Jesus ... he ... worshipped him,

Mark 5:6

The madman of Gadara ran to Jesus and worshipped Him. A few minutes later, this mad man was resisting his deliverance. This is a mystery, which must be understood. It seems that it is possible for demons to invade a godly man and be compatible.

I asked myself, "How can these two extreme forces be compatible? How can a man with a legion of demons worship God?" The man with a legion of demons was a worshipper of Christ Jesus. "How can a man who runs to Jesus be full of demons?"

Today, how many Christians run to worship the Lord? They come strolling into church saying in their minds, "You are lucky I came to church today!" But not so with the mad man of Gadara; he ran to Jesus!

This phenomenon explains how many Christians come to church every Sunday and yet have evil spirits influencing them at home and at work.

A Worshipper with Demons

The man in the synagogue was another worshipper who had a demon. The demon was exposed as the preaching came forth.

And there was in their synagogue a man with an unclean spirit; and he cried out, Saying, Let us alone; what have we to do with thee, thou Jesus of Nazareth? Art thou come to destroy us? I know thee who thou art, the Holy One of God.

Mark 1:23-24

As you can see, churchgoers and worshippers may have evil spirits in them.

Satan and the Apostle

The Apostle Peter was moved by the Holy Spirit to say that Jesus was the Christ, the Son of God. Yet a few minutes later, Satan was rebuked in his life. In a surprising and stunning turn, gentle Jesus turned into a Jesus of steel and said, " Satan get thee behind me."

And Simon Peter answered and said, Thou art the Christ, the Son of the living God. And Jesus answered and said unto him, BLESSED ART THOU, SIMON BAR-JONA: FOR FLESH AND BLOOD HATH NOT REVEALED IT UNTO THEE, but my Father which is in heaven.

Then Peter took him, and began to rebuke him, saying, Be it far from thee, Lord: this shall not be unto thee. But he turned, and SAID UNTO PETER, GET THEE BEHIND ME, SATAN: thou art an offence unto me: for thou savourest not the things that be of God, but those that be of men.

Matthew 16:16-17,22-23

Samson is another example of someone who had the Spirit of God moving in him.

And the woman bare a son, and CALLED HIS NAME SAMSON: and the child grew, and the LORD blessed him. AND THE SPIRIT OF THE LORD BEGAN TO MOVE HIM...

Judges 13:24-25

Unfortunately, this did not stop the spirit of fornication from operating in his ministry. This phenomenon explains how some ministers seem to be very anointed and also troubled by evil spirits.

Some prophets have amazing gifts and yet are subject to the influence of evil spirits.

Chapter 16

Demons Operate from a Spiritual Distance and Not a Physical Distance

The confusion over the apparent compatibility of the Holy Spirit and the forces of darkness can be explained by this principle.

When something is physically close it does not mean that it is spiritually close by. In other words, one thousand miles of distance in the natural does not mean one thousand miles in the spirit. Something may be next door in the natural but thousands of spiritual miles away.

This is why someone can be close to a spiritual person but not be affected by the anointing on his life. He is physically close but spiritually far away! Someone else may be thousands of miles away and receive a greater blessing than someone nearby.

Jesus said, "A prophet is not accepted in his own home." This means that the gifts of the prophets are unable to spiritually affect people who are nearby. The prophet's gift and anointing seems to work on people who are physically further from him. Somehow familiarity increases the spiritual distance between the anointed and the one who has to receive the anointing. And they were offended in him. But Jesus said unto them, A prophet is not without honour, save in his own country, and in his own house.

And they were offended in him. But Jesus said unto them, A prophet is not without honour, save in his own country, and in his own house.

Matthew 13:57

I find that the anointing of the Lord flows more easily from my life into the lives of people who are further away from me physically. *Many who are near in the natural are far in the spirit.*

This proves the theory that spiritual distance and natural distance are different things.

Spiritual Distance

There is something like distance within the realm of the spirit. Jesus once said to a man who came to Him, "You are not far from the Kingdom."

And when Jesus saw that he answered discreetly, he said unto him, THOU ART NOT FAR FROM THE KINGDOM OF GOD...

Mark 12:34

This saying proves that you can be far or near to the Kingdom. Other Scriptures speak of drawing near to God. Drawing near to God is not a physical thing. God is a spirit, and cannot be approached by any physical or natural manoeuver. Sitting next to the man of God does not make you near to him spiritually. In fact, someone sitting six thousand miles away may be closer than you sitting at his feet.

Blessed is the man whom thou choosest, and causest to approach unto thee, that he may dwell in thy courts: we shall be satisfied with the goodness of thy house, even of thy holy temple.

Psalm 65:4

This Scripture speaks of the blessing of a man who is allowed to approach God. God chooses those He will allow to come near. Some people are nearer to God than others! We may all be physically located in New York City, but God's close friends and servants may be only five spiritual metres away from the presence of God. Whereas another Christian, also in New York City may be five thousand miles from the presence of God.

Being physically near to a shrine or a witch's house does not mean you are near to these evil things in the spirit. You are spiritually far from them unless you open yourself up to them. Give no place to the devil!

The same person can be filled with the spirit of God and within a few minutes be controlled by evil spirits. This happens because within a few minutes, this same person may move very far spiritually although he is physically in the same position. This is what happened to Peter and it explains how Jesus called him "the rock" and a few minutes later called him "Satan".

I remember reading a story about a minister of God switching between two spirits, from a book by Kenneth Hagin. Kenneth Hagin said that he was holding a meeting in a certain city and staying in the home of a wealthy businessman who was a member of the church where he was ministering. This man owned a shopping centre and was extremely successful in business.

The businessman asked Kenneth Hagin whether he knew a certain brother who was also a minister. Kenneth Hagin said that he knew about the man and was convinced that he was called of God and walked uprightly before God in the ministry, until he began yielding to wrong spirits.

The businessman told Kenneth Hagin that their church had helped sponsor this minister in a meeting in their town and that nearly everyday, this minister would come into his office and they would talk or go out to lunch.

This businessman had an heirloom--a seven-carat diamond ring, that he had inherited from his father, which he seldom ever wore. He had wrapped it in a handkerchief in the back right corner of the chest of drawers in his bedroom.

This minister of God went into the businessman's office and told him about this heirloom given to the businessman by his father. He described in detail to the businessman where the heirloom was kept and told him that God wanted the heirloom given to him.. The businessman had naturally thought it was from God because it was supernatural knowledge, and consequently he had given the heirloom to the minister.

But this businessman had been worried about the fact that this minister of God had started cursing when someone had made him cross in his office. Moreover shortly after he had left town, two men had approached him that while the minister was in town, he had been involved in homosexuality.

He had been angry with himself for giving his heirloom to someone he thought was not even walking with God.

Reverend Hagin said in his book that the spirit of God had whispered to him that this man of God was operating in occult powers and familiar spirits when he later met him at a meeting. This minister had in the past had a marvellous healing ministry with some of his supernatural healings attested to by medical doctors. He had however yielded to the flesh and opened himself up to the devil.

As you can see from this story, the man of God was operating by the Holy Spirit and then by familiar spirits.

Chapter 17

Demons Seek to Influence Human Beings by Thoughts, Imaginations and Suggestions

Casting down IMAGINATIONS, and every ...
THOUGHT...

2 Corinthians 10:5

Satan's entry into our lives is through the power of suggestion. When Jesus was attacked by Satan in the wilderness, He had to defend Himself against clever suggestions. The suggestions of demons come in three categories. You must be aware of these three categories of satanic attacks that come to all of us.

Type 1 Suggestion: The suggestion to yield to fleshly desires.

And the devil said unto him, If thou be the Son of God, command this stone that it BE MADE BREAD.

Luke 4:3

We are constantly urged by the voice of Satan to succumb to our flesh. Jesus was hungry after forty days of fasting. The devil urged Him to follow His flesh. The voice that urges you to sleep on, to break your fast and to do immoral things is the voice of Satan. Do not be deceived; this is the first and basic entry point of demons into your life.

Type 2 Suggestion: The suggestion to worship and serve something other than God. This is also a suggestion to choose the quick and easy route to your goal.

And the devil said unto him, All this power will I give thee, and the glory of them: for that is delivered unto me; and to whomsoever I will I give it. If thou therefore wilt worship me, all shall be thine.

Luke 4:6-7

Countless Christians are urged to live for money and other earthly achievements. It is the voice of no other than Satan which urges you to spend your life, your time, your energy and your money on everything but God's work.

Satan will not mind if you spend your money on politics, football, clothes etc. Some people think that what I am saying is too strong. But Satan hides in the darkness and uses Christians and righteous looking people to do his work.

Do you remember when Peter said to Jesus, "You will not die on this terrible cross; we will do everything to prevent you from having such an unpleasant experience?" That was the first and only time Jesus rebuked him publicly. Unfortunately, decent Peter had been used by Satan to suggest the need for self-preservation. Jesus showed us that men's craving for self-preservation is of the devil.

From that time forth began Jesus to shew unto his disciples, how that he must go unto Jerusalem, and suffer many things of the elders and chief priests and scribes, and be killed, and be raised again the third day.

Then Peter took him, and began to rebuke him, saying, Be it far from thee, Lord: this shall not be unto thee. But he turned, and SAID UNTO PETER, GET THEE BEHIND ME, SATAN: thou art an offence unto me: FOR THOU SAVOUREST NOT THE THINGS THAT BE OF GOD, BUT THOSE THAT BE OF MEN.
Matthew 16:21-23

The things that men value are often things that are not of God. Please take note of this for your personal life. Perhaps men are urging you to do certain things but God is urging you to die for Him. We must have the character of Christ. We must take up our crosses and follow Jesus to Calvary.

We must embrace the plan of God and not follow the deceptions of Satan.

Die Like a Lamb or Die Like a Pig?

Christ died with the calmness of a lamb. He embraced the will of God with peace. Most Christians die for the Lord like pigs—with a lot of squealing and reluctance. Have you ever seen a pig being slaughtered? We reluctantly embrace the will of God with a lot of squealing, screaming and resistance. Receive the lamb-like nature of our Saviour, Jesus Christ!

Type 3 Suggestion: The suggestion to misuse the gifts and blessings of God.

And he brought him to Jerusalem, and set him on a pinnacle of the temple, and said unto him, If thou be the Son of God, cast thyself down from hence: For it is written, He shall give his angels charge over thee, to keep thee:

Luke 4:9-10

Jesus had the power to use the gift of God to protect Himself. Was He going to misuse this power at the suggestion of demons? Certainly not! This common category of suggestion seeks to make you misuse whatever God has placed in your hand. God has given some of us spiritual gifts, callings, money, talents, education, contacts, power and influence.

Most people with these gifts from God misuse them. Satan cleverly suggests that we use our God-given blessings on anything other than the will of God. This is why many blessed Christians do not support the work of God whole-heartedly but they support their own lives! This also explains why many men of God deviate from the call and misuse the gift of God.

The power of suggestion seems weak and insignificant but this is the principal access route of demons. I remember reading a very powerful vision of a pastor's wife who encountered exactly what I am talking about.

She received a type one suggestion from the devil.

In this vision, Jesus appeared to Kenneth Hagin and talked to him extensively on the subject of demons and how they get hold of people. In the vision, Jesus told Kenneth Hagin that He was going to teach him concerning the devil, demons and demon possession. Jesus then opened the realm of the spirit to Kenneth Hagin and he saw a woman whom he recognized but did not know personally.

This lady was a pastor's wife who was in the ministry with her husband. She had a great singing ability but she had left her husband and gone off on her way.

Jesus explained to Kenneth Hagin that this woman was a child of God until one day the devil came to her. As Jesus said this, Kenneth Hagin saw in the spirit, what looked like a little monkey come to sit on the shoulder of this pastor's wife and whisper something in her ear.

Jesus told Kenneth Hagin that the demon told the pastor's wife that she was a beautiful woman who had been robbed in life and that if she were in the world she would have fame, fortune and popularity. In the vision, the woman recognized the thought as coming from the devil and so she rebuked the demon and as she did so, Kenneth Hagin saw the little monkey jump off her shoulder and run off.

Jesus told Kenneth Hagin that by and by this demon came back to sit on the woman's shoulder and whisper, the same thing to her. Every time, this pastor's wife would recognize the voice of the devil and rebuke it and the demon would go away.

Jesus continued His narration to Kenneth Hagin and said that after a while, the demon came back to tempt the woman. As Jesus said this, Kenneth Hagin saw in the vision this little imp come again to sit on the shoulder of this pastor's wife and whisper something to her.

Jesus told Kenneth Hagin that at this time, the pastor's wife began to think Satan's thoughts as well. She began to think that she was beautiful and that she had been cheated in life. Jesus continued to explain to Kenneth Hagin that when the pastor's wife began to think like that, she became obsessed with the devil's thoughts. As Jesus said this, Kenneth Hagin saw in the spirit that the pastor's wife changed and became transparent as if her body was made of glass. Then he saw a black dot in her head about the size of a half-dollar coin.

Jesus explained to Kenneth Hagin that before, the devil oppressed this woman from outside but as she listened to the devil she became obsessed with the devil's thoughts. Jesus told Kenneth Hagin how this pastor's wife eventually left her husband and went off with another man. She went from one man to another until at a time she had been with five different men.

As the vision continued, Kenneth Hagin saw a minister of God, standing outside a hotel where this pastor's wife was lodging with another man. He had gone there to reconcile the pastor's wife back to her husband.

In the vision, Kenneth Hagin found himself appearing in the hallway by this minister when he knocked on the door of the hotel room where the pastor's wife was lodging with her partner. He saw her in the vision, come to the door with almost no clothes on. She drove away the minister saying that she knew what he had come for and that she did not want to have anything to do with Jesus.

When she said that, Kenneth Hagin saw in the spirit that big black dot in her head, go from her head down inside of her, into her heart and down into her spirit. Jesus told Kenneth Hagin that at that point, the woman had become possessed with that devil.

What the devil had originally brought to this woman as a suggestion, embedded itself in her mind, and eventually possessed her heart and spirit. This illustrates how Satan used the power of suggestion until this woman was totally destroyed.

Right and Wrong Thinking

This is why the Bible teaches exactly what we must think about. The mind is the battlefield for your soul. When the wrong thoughts become established in your mind, you suffer from deceptions and delusions. Satan then uses these delusions to destroy you. It is important to constantly cast down imaginations that are contrary to the will of God.

(For the weapons of our warfare are not carnal, but mighty through God to the pulling down of strong holds)
2 Corinthians 10:4

You must also control the pattern of thinking in your mind. Your thoughts must pass the Philippians 4:8 test before they are allowed to stay. Thoughts are like birds, they can fly over your head. But you can prevent them from building their nests over your head.

Finally, brethren, whatsoever things are true, whatsoever things are honest, whatsoever things are just, whatsoever things are pure, whatsoever things are lovely, whatsoever things are of good report; if there be any virtue, and if there be any praise, think on these things.
Philippians 4:8

Chapter 18

Demons Cause Physical Changes in Human Beings

...had been often bound with fetters and chains...and NO
MAN HAD STRENGTH TO TAME HIM.

Mark 5:4 (ASV)

And there were seven sons of one Sceva, a Jew, and chief
of the priests, which did so. And the evil spirit answered
and said, Jesus I know, and Paul I know; but who are
ye? And the MAN IN WHOM THE EVIL SPIRIT WAS
LEAPED ON THEM, AND OVERCAME THEM, and
PREVAILED AGAINST THEM, so that they fled out of
that house naked and wounded.

Acts 19:14-16

From these two testimonies, we see that the presence of demons gave unnatural human strength. One mad man was able to beat up seven men. That is supernatural strength. The mad man of Gadara was able to break chains. It is not natural to be able to break chains with your bare hands. Even the weight lifting champions do not break chains with their bare hands.

This principle provides a very important revelation of the effect that evil spirits have on our physical lives. Evil spirits want to inhabit a human body so that they can affect the person physically. Sickness can be caused by the presence of evil spirits in your body. When you open your life to evil spirits, they can fasten themselves to your body and cause illness.

I read two powerful testimonies from one of Kenneth Hagin's books, which illustrate this principle perfectly. In one of them, a twenty-three year old woman suffering from cancer of the lungs was healed when the demon was cast away. She had been brought to a meeting that Reverend Hagin was holding in a certain town, to be prayed for.

As Kenneth Hagin laid hands on her, he suddenly was enveloped in a glory cloud and he saw a little creature which looked like a monkey hanging onto a tree limb, on the outside of the woman's body.

This monkey-like creature was holding on to the woman's left lung where the cancer had started. Reverend Hagin commanded the demon to leave but it refused to go. Then Kenneth Hagin commanded it to leave in the name of the Lord Jesus Christ and it fell off the lady's body. It whimpered, and whined and shook like a beaten pup.

Then Kenneth Hagin commanded it to leave the premises and he saw this creature run out of the aisle and walk out of the door.

This lady was completely healed afterwards. That same week she went to see the doctors and they told her that her lungs had been completely healed and marvelled, asking her how it happened.

In the second testimony, a pastor's wife with cancer of the breast was healed as an evil spirit came out of her. The cancer had started in the lady's left breast and had spread to her lymph glands. By the time she got to the doctor, it was too late and they could not do anything for her.

Kenneth Hagin went with his wife and another pastor to pray for her. They continued praying for this lady for two days and two nights. Suddenly, the Holy Spirit told them to go and stand at the head of the bed and command the spirit of doubt and fear to leave. The moment Kenneth Hagin did that, he saw a great black bat, twice as big as a man's hand, just rise up from that dying woman's left breast and fly out of the window.

The woman instantly rose up completely healed. She praised God and danced all over the house. She was totally delivered and set free.

Is it not amazing how the presence of a demon can cause cancer?

When Demons Cause Epilepsy

And one of the multitude answered and said, Master, I have brought unto thee my son, which hath a dumb spirit; And wheresoever he taketh him, he teareth him: and he foameth, and gnasheth with his teeth, and pineth away: and I spake to thy disciples that they should cast him out; and they could not. He answereth him, and saith, O faithless generation, how long shall I be with you? how long shall I suffer you? bring him unto me.
And they brought him unto him: and when he saw him, STRAIGHTWAY THE SPIRIT TARE HIM; AND HE FELL ON THE GROUND, AND WALLOWED FOAMING.

And he asked his father, How long is it ago since this came unto him? And he said, Of a child. And ofttimes it hath cast him into the fire, and into the waters, to destroy him: but if thou canst do any thing, have compassion on us, and help us. Jesus said unto him, If thou canst believe, all things are possible to him that believeth.

And straightway the father of the child cried out, and said with tears, Lord, I believe; help thou mine unbelief. When Jesus saw that the people came running together, he rebuked the foul spirit, saying unto him, Thou dumb and deaf spirit, I charge thee, come out of him, and enter no more into him. And the spirit cried, and rent him sore, and came out of him: and he was as one dead; insomuch that many said, He is dead. But Jesus took him by the hand, and lifted him up; and he arose. And when he was come into the house, his disciples asked him privately, Why could not we cast him out? And he said unto them, This kind can come forth by nothing, but by prayer and fasting.

Mark 9:17-29

The presence of the evil spirit made the young man experience chronic convulsions. The evil spirit made him throw himself into the fire. The presence of evil spirits causes all kinds of physical illnesses.

Evil spirits can cause barrenness! Evil spirits cause cancers! Evil spirits cause heart diseases! Evil spirits cause mental illnesses! You should always deal with evil spirits as led by the Spirit of God.

Screaming and Rolling

Some people do not understand why people writhe and scream when demons are going out of them. But the Scripture shows that as Philip ministered, evil spirits came out screaming.

Then Philip went down to the city of Samaria, and preached Christ unto them. And the people with one accord gave heed unto those things which Philip spake, hearing and seeing the miracles which he did. FOR UNCLEAN SPIRITS, CRYING WITH LOUD VOICE, came out of many that were possessed with them: and many taken with palsies, and that were lame, were healed. And there was great joy in that city.

Acts 8:5-8

Screaming and rolling over, are common biblical occurrences. They are signs of evil spirits going out of human beings.

Living Deliciously

There are other physical manifestations of the presence of evil spirits. Some evil spirits cause an accentuation of lustful behaviour. Some people under the influence of evil spirits, are trapped in extreme lustful and immoral behaviour. An unnatural desire and practice of sexuality leads them into all kinds of experiences.

The prophets bewailed Babylon because she had become the habitation of evil spirits. When these evil spirits inhabited

Babylon what happened? She committed fornication, lived deliciously, and glorified herself.

And he cried mightily with a strong voice, saying, Babylon the great is fallen, is fallen, and is become the habitation of devils, and the hold of every foul spirit, and a cage of every unclean and hateful bird.

How much she hath glorified herself, and LIVED DELICIOUSLY, so much torment and sorrow give her: for she saith in her heart, I sit a queen, and am no widow, and shall see no sorrow.

And the kings of the earth, WHO HAVE COMMITTED FORNICATION AND LIVED DELICIOUSLY WITH HER, shall bewail her, and lament for her, when they shall see the smoke of her burning,
Revelation 18:2,7,9

How the Birds Came

Babylon is described as a hold for every unclean bird. It is described as a woman who has become the habitation of foul spirits.

And he cried mightily with a strong voice, saying, Babylon the great is fallen, is fallen, and is become the habitation of devils, and the hold of every foul spirit, and a cage of every unclean and hateful bird.
Revelation 18:2

But how did these evil spirits come into her in the first place? The Bible gives us the answer. It explains that these evil spirits came because many people drank from the wine of her fornication.

Evil spirits inhabit men and women who give themselves over to fornication with multiple partners (the nations). These evil spirits inhabit the individuals and cause them to live deliciously (immorally) for a season of their lives. Often when these individuals become older and less sexually active, the evil spirits leave them for other younger candidates. Many of these individuals would never reveal the depth to which these lustful spirits have taken them.

Nations and Demons

The pleasurable lifestyles of some nations are often a manifestation of demons in those countries. In certain nations, evil spirits sometimes cause the physical appearance of dirt and underdevelopment. These people are resistant to all forms of improvement. Unrelenting wars in many nations also show demon activity.

Dear Christian friend, evil spirits do have an effect on your physical body. These effects may influence you to indulge in fleshly sins or to be violent. Evil spirits may also cause strange illnesses to fasten themselves onto a believer. The time of ignorance is past. We are no longer ignorant of the wiles of the devil.

Chapter 19

Demons Are Challenged by the Presence of God

When he saw Jesus, he cried out,... I beseech thee, torment me not.

Luke 8:28

When Jesus came on the scene, the demons within the mad man were agitated. They cried out against the Lord.

The presence of God is the environment which evil spirits are not comfortable with. The mad man of Gadara reacted to the presence of Jesus. The presence of God will always stir up evil spirits. That is why perfectly normal people suddenly show strange manifestations when they are in church.

In Mark 1, a perfectly normal person began screaming in the temple while Jesus was preaching.

And there was in their synagogue a man with an unclean spirit; AND HE CRIED OUT, Saying, Let us alone; what have we to do with thee, thou Jesus of Nazareth? art thou come to destroy us? I know thee who thou art, the Holy One of God. And Jesus rebuked him, saying, Hold thy peace, and come out of him. And when the unclean spirit had torn him, and cried with a loud voice, he came out of him.

Mark 1:23-26

When you understand that the presence of God drives away evil spirits, you will constantly cultivate the presence of God in your life. You will want the presence of God at home, in your office, and at church.

There are two reasons why the presence of God stirs up evil spirits.

1. **In the presence of God, the Word of God is preached and taught.**

The Word of God is a sharp sword.

For the word of God is quick, and powerful, and SHARPER THAN ANY TWOEDGED SWORD...

Hebrews 4:12

As the Word of God comes forth, swords are thrown out in the realm of the spirit. No demon enjoys having swords thrown at him. This is why the man in the synagogue reacted to the preaching of Jesus. Jesus did not pray, He just preached. Jesus did not bind any demon; He just preached the Word of God. The Word of God is truly a sword in the spirit.

2. **The Word of God is light and the light exposes the activities of demons.**

And the light shineth in darkness; and the darkness comprehended it not.

John 1:5

When the Word is preached, the light shines forth and demons are exposed. The more of the Word you have, the more the enemy is exposed. Satan can never operate effectively against you in the light. Darkness is essential for demonic activity.

Creating Your Own Atmosphere

The Bible teaches that God inhabits praises. When praise and worship goes on, the presence of God becomes very strong and the evil spirits feel the fire.

But thou art holy, O thou that INHABITEST THE PRAISES of Israel.

Psalm 22:3

It is possible to create a church environment everywhere. You can do this by carrying your worship tapes and CDs wherever you go. You can have them in your home or in your car or in your office. Many surgeons play music while they operate.

Why not play worship music while you work?

You can also carry preaching tapes with you wherever you go. Preaching and worship are the two main items for creating the right atmosphere. Wherever I go, I carry my music and my preaching tapes. From Paraguay, to Toronto, I always create my own atmosphere with preaching tapes and worship music. This environment is anti-demonic.

Many people suffer from depression because they do not know how to create the right atmosphere for their lives. Instead of having worship music, they listen to secular music from the radio. Instead of listening to preaching, they listen to political discussions and the bad news of the world.

Music and the Presence of God

Unfortunately, many Christians do not know the effect that music has on evil spirits. There are four biblical accounts, which warn us about playing with the wrong music.

1. Satan, once called Lucifer, was created to worship God. Music was actually ingrained in him when he was formed. Lucifer was created with timbrels and pipes. Since he fell, this gift of music has been corrupted and used to fight against God.

Every Christian must be careful of secular music no matter how harmless it appears. Christian musicians must not play secular music if they want to be truly spiritual. Have you ever wondered at the kind of Christian music produced today? I have heard many spiritual people declare that they find it difficult to listen to some so-called gospel music.

You were in Eden, the garden of God; Every precious stone was your covering: The sardius, topaz, and diamond, Beryl, onyx, and jasper, Sapphire, turquoise, and emerald with gold. THE WORKMANSHIP OF YOUR TIMBRELS AND PIPES WAS PREPARED FOR YOU ON THE DAY YOU WERE CREATED.
Ezekiel 28:13 (New King James Version)

2. When King Saul was tormented by an evil spirit, instrumental music was used to drive away the demons.

But the Spirit of the LORD departed from Saul, and an evil spirit from the LORD troubled him. And Saul's servants said unto him, Behold now, an evil spirit from God troubleth thee. Let our Lord now command thy servants, which are before thee, to seek out a man, who is a cunning player on an harp: and it shall come to pass, when the evil spirit from God is upon thee, that he shall play with his hand, and thou shalt be well. And Saul said unto his servants, Provide me now a man that can play well, and bring him to me. Then answered one of the servants, and said, Behold, I have seen a son of Jesse the Bethlehemite, that is cunning in playing, and a mighty valiant man, and a man of war, and prudent in matters, and a comely person, and the LORD is with him.

Wherefore Saul sent messengers unto Jesse, and said, Send me David thy son, which is with the sheep. And Jesse took an ass laden with bread, and a bottle of wine, and a kid, and sent them by David his son unto Saul. And David came to Saul, and stood before him: and he loved him greatly; and he became his armourbearer. And Saul sent to Jesse, saying, Let David, I pray thee, stand before me; for he hath found favour in my sight. AND IT CAME TO PASS, WHEN THE EVIL SPIRIT FROM GOD WAS UPON SAUL, THAT DAVID TOOK AN HARP, AND PLAYED WITH HIS HAND: SO SAUL WAS REFRESHED, AND WAS WELL, AND THE EVIL SPIRIT DEPARTED FROM HIM.

1 Samuel 16:14-23

Dear friend, if music can drive away demons, surely it is able to attract them too! Be careful about what you listen to because it may attract demons to your life. Much of the unspiritual gospel music is charged with evil spirits. People are charged with spirits of lust and violence when they listen to certain kinds of music.

**All things are lawful for me, but all things are not
expedient: all things are lawful for me, but all things edify
not.**

1 Corinthians 10:23

3. When Elisha needed to hear from the Spirit of God, he called
    for the minstrel. As the minstrel played, the Spirit of God
    came upon him and he prophesied.

    **And Elisha said ... now bring me a minstrel. And it
    came to pass, when the minstrel played, that the hand of
    the LORD came upon him. And he said, Thus saith the
    LORD, Make this valley full of ditches.**

2 Kings 3:14-16

Surely, this testimony must teach you something: The right
music can attract the presence of God!

4. When the musicians in the temple played instruments
    and worshipped God, the presence of God filled the house.

    **It came even to pass, AS THE TRUMPETERS AND
    SINGERS WERE AS ONE, to make one sound to be
    heard in praising and thanking the LORD; and when they
    lifted up their voice with the trumpets and cymbals and
    instruments of musick, and praised the LORD, saying,
    For he is good; for his mercy endureth for ever: that then
    THE HOUSE WAS FILLED WITH A CLOUD, EVEN
    THE HOUSE OF THE LORD;**

2 Chronicles 5:13

The glory cloud came in because musicians and singers were
doing the right thing. Surely, we must learn from this account
that the right kind of singing and the right kind of instrumental
music will bring in the presence of God. Many times, I have
felt the presence of God as I listened to anointed and inspired
music. Music is truly a powerful medium that takes you into the
presence of God.

Chapter 20

Identify the Demons

And Jesus asked him sayiing, WHAT IS THY NAME? ... he said, Legion...

Luke 8:30

In the medical field, 80% of your work is done when you are able to identify what disease you are dealing with. The difficulty is often in being able to determine what the problem is. There are many elusive diseases, which avoid diagnoses. These are the most difficult diseases to treat. In the same way, demons and demonic activity must be identified (diagnosed), in order to be able to deal with them.

Perhaps you think you are dealing with a spirit of fornication but actually you may be dealing with a spirit of death. As soon as you can pin point the problem, you are well on your way to a breakthrough. If I were to scream, "Come here," perhaps no one in particular would come to me. However, if I were to scream, "Jack Toronto, come here", Jack Toronto would get up and come to me.

In both cases, I said, "Come here." One of the commands yielded results but the other did not. Specifically mentioning the name of the problem and dealing with it, is the key to dealing with demonic powers. That is why Jesus asked the mad man of Gadara: "What is thy name?" He needed to call out the name of the spirit to be able to cast it out.

Begin to mention the names of the spirits that are harassing you. Ask God to reveal the real identity of the spirits.

Once while I was praying, the Lord revealed the names of some demons I was dealing with. In one case, the Lord told me that the name of the problem was "death". He went on to show me that Satan was trying to kill me by using some of my pastors.

We need to ask God for the Holy Spirit so that we can deal with the enemy.

What is thy name? What is thy name? What is thy name? This is the most important question to ask when dealing with demons.

Chapter 21

Demons Lose Their Hold When You Disagree with Them

But when he saw Jesus afar off, he ran and worshipped him...

Mark 5:6

In one lucid moment, the mad man of Gadara broke out of the control of the demons and ran to worship Jesus. Satan seeks to gain control over us. The only way he can do this is through our minds.

And the devil said unto him,...command this stone that it be made bread... Jesus answered ... man shall not live by bread alone...

Luke 4:3-4

Now the serpent was more subtil than any beast of the field which the LORD God had made. And he said unto the woman, Yea, hath God said, Ye shall not eat of every tree of the garden? And the woman said unto the serpent, We may eat of the fruit of the trees of the garden:

But of the fruit of the tree which is in the midst of the garden, God hath said, Ye shall not eat of it, neither shall ye touch it, lest ye die. And the serpent said unto the woman, Ye shall not surely die: For God doth know that in the day ye eat thereof, then your eyes shall be opened, and ye shall be as gods, knowing good and evil. And when the woman saw that the tree was good for food, and that it was pleasant to the eyes, and a tree to be desired to make one wise, she took of the fruit thereof, and did eat, and gave also unto her husband with her; and he did eat.

Genesis 3:1-6

Many people are held in bondage because their thinking pattern agrees with demonic deceptions. People are kept in bondage as long as their minds agree with the ideas that come

77

from Satan. Unfortunately, the thoughts of many believers are in agreement with Satan because we do not study or believe the Word.

When a person is full of thoughts of discontentment and criticism, the demon of hatred can easily take over. Our natural thoughts for revenge, unforgiveness, depression and fear are very much in consonance with the spirit of sickness, disease and even death. This is why the Word of God is so important. It keeps us in full disagreement with the devil's suggestions.

It is very easy to agree with delusions of demons. The devil's deceptions are very similar to the truth. Many times, we are caught unawares as we drift along and agree with unbiblical suggestions.

That is where steadfastness comes in. Steadfastness is actually derived from a navy term, which means to stay on course. It also means to come back to course after you have made a deviation.

We all tend to go on excursions from time to time but the spirit of steadfastness must bring us back to the Word. Put your foot down and disagree with everything that is not biblical.

Chapter 22

Demons Are Persistent

And when the devil had ended all the temptation, HE DEPARTED FROM HIM FOR A SEASON.

Luke 4:13

Satan is a very persistent being. In the temptation of Jesus, he left the Lord only for a season. Any time you are dealing with a demonic attack, you must be aware of this nature of persistence. You must counteract it with an even more persistent determination to be free.

Jesus was tempted in the wilderness to take a short cut to His ministry. Satan asked Jesus to bow down and worship him so that he would give Him the whole world. It was a quick way to win the whole world, instead of having to suffer. Some years later, Satan came through Peter and opposed the idea of suffering on the cross.

From that time forth began Jesus to shew unto his disciples, how that he must go unto Jerusalem, and suffer many things of the elders and chief priests and scribes, and be killed, and be raised again the third day. Then Peter took him, and began to rebuke him, saying, Be it far from thee, Lord: this shall not be unto thee.

Matthew 16:21-22

Once again, Jesus had to rebuke Satan. Even later, Pontius Pilate asked Jesus, "Do you not know that I have the ability to set you free?"

Then saith Pilate unto him, Speakest thou not unto me? knowest thou not that I have power to crucify thee, and have power to release thee?

John 19:10

This was another suggestion that Jesus could avoid the cross. Even while Christ was on the cross, men wagged their heads and suggested that He came down from the cross to prove that He is the Son of God.

Likewise also the chief priests mocking said among themselves with the scribes, He saved others; himself he cannot save. Let Christ the King of Israel descend now from the cross, that we may see and believe. And they that were crucified with him reviled him.

Mark 15:31-32

Satan never gave up until Jesus died. Satan will never give up until you and I are dead. You may be seventy years old but he may still try to deceive you. We are dealing with a persistent enemy.

God has given us the tenacity of a mountain goat, the eye of an eagle, the heart of a lion, the endurance of a camel, the strength of a horse and the steadfastness of a shark! We are more than able to resist the onslaught of the devil.

Someone asked me when he would be free from the devil's attacks. I said to him, "Only when you are dead." He was shocked but that is the truth.

In my own life and ministry, I have watched as Satan has persisted in his attacks against my life. Satan has been relentless and unyielding in his onslaught. He shamelessly returns with the same problem after a season of respite. Sometimes he gives the problem a new look but it is the same problem repackaged and represented. Don't let the persistent nature of problems discourage you. That is the nature of the enemy we are dealing with. Rise up with the tenacity of a mountain goat, and prevail over your enemy today.

Chapter 23

Snakes and Pastors

Unfortunately, demons have also infiltrated the ranks of pastors and Christian leadership. There are certain spirits that greatly affect ministers. Please take note of this list of demons commonly found working among pastors and Christian leaders. It will help us all to identify and resist the enemy within our ranks.

1. Self-Promotion

2. Lust

3. Pride

4. Insecurity

5. The Fear of Man

6. Jealousy

7. Bitterness

8. Religion

9. Tradition

10. The Spirit of Discouragement

11. Depression

An amazing vision related by Scott MacLeod illustrates the activities of demons amongst men of God. It is amazing how Satan creeps into our midst and works against the ministry. In the book of Job, we read how Satan came into the midst of the gathering of the sons of God. Satan has always wanted to be in the midst of the brethren to accuse, to divide and to deceive. His desire is to dwell amongst us and cause confusion. His title "accuser in the midst of the brethren", is most apt. He is able to turn the closest of friends against each other.

Now there was a day when the sons of God came to present themselves before the LORD, and SATAN CAME ALSO AMONG THEM.

Job 1:6

I want to share a vision that I believe is truly revealing. It is indeed scary that our greatest enemy can infiltrate to the highest level. I believe you will be blessed as you read this account by Scott MacCleod in his book "Snakes in the Lobby".

The Lobby

This is the vision: I was standing in a well-known hotel lobby, which I had literally stood in earlier that same day during a very well-known Christian music conference. In the vision the very large and open lobby was packed full, as it usually is, with men and women from all over. Many were artists, musicians or people directly involved in the business of music. The people were busy talking and going on with their business (what is commonly called 'schmoozing'), each one dressed up in appropriate music attire.

Much to my astonishment and horror, I saw what looked like a massive snake lying on the lobby floor. I could not even begin to calculate its length, but it easily covered the full length of the room. Its fat middle was at least six feet in height and looked almost twenty feet in width. It looked totally stuffed. Amazingly, people were actually leaning up against it!

I could hardly believe what I was seeing. My first impulse was to yell and warn everyone, but I hesitated because no one else seemed to notice it—they just carried on with their business. Many people were surrounded, and some were even totally wrapped up in its monstrous coils, and yet they were still unaware. They all were in great danger. I couldn't tell if the people could not see what I was seeing, or if they had simply grown accustomed to this monster. It almost seemed welcome here.

I wondered, "Who let this thing in here? Surely the thing has to be dead for people to be standing this close to it and still be this comfortable with it."

Then it happened... IT MOVED. I couldn't believe that something that looked so heavy could actually move. But it did. It slowly poured itself in between a few groups of preoccupied people so as not to disturb anyone. It was silent, and no one saw it move. No one seemed to have a sense of danger. This was extremely confusing to me. It looked like many in this place, for some reason, had totally dropped their guard. Obviously, this seemed crazy because of what I was seeing. As I stood there, greatly perplexed by this strange scenario, I was suddenly struck with the terrifying sense that there were other snakes in the room.

I reluctantly and cautiously gazed across the room. We were surrounded! The oversized serpents were everywhere! As I continued to observe the situation, my emotions began to evolve rapidly from initial shock and terror into great frustration because no one else seemed to be aware of these snakes. Soon I was filled with a sense of compassion for the blinded victims, and finally an intense anger gripped me because these creatures had somehow infiltrated this place.

That was it. That was all I saw at first. But I knew immediately that the great snakes I had seen in this vision were the principalities and dark powers (or evil spirits) that have been controlling and manipulating much of Christian music. I knew I had seen exactly what the small group of us had just been praying about, and I told them what I had seen. It was as if a small movie screen had appeared before me and shown me these things, in color.

The vision stayed with me for about 24 hours. I was surprised that it did. I guess I had hoped that what I had seen at first was the end of it, for it was not pleasant to dwell on. But it remained very graphic and the images would not go away. After starting to get literally sick to my stomach over what I had seen, my curiosity began to grow and I began wondering what the meaning of it was.

Believing there had to be a reason for this lingering scene, I finally began to ask the Lord to show me the full meaning of the vision.

He did, and this is what was revealed next:

The Big One: Self Promotion

I was taken back to the same lobby and was shown each snake in vivid detail.

The first snake that was revealed to me was the first one that I had seen earlier, it was definitely the biggest one, easily filling the full length of the large lobby with its great coils wrapped around everywhere. This grayish colored snake was so large that it took me quite some time to find its huge head. I finally spotted the head hiding in the twisted masses of the mammoth coils. It had a hollow and yet all consuming look upon its face. One word came into my mind as I studied its massive head - HUNGER. I then observed that it had just finished devouring something, or someone. I instinctively knew it was the latter. This snake was actually feeding on the people in the lobby and still no one seemed to notice!

This serpent had the ability to slowly surround its victims with enormous coils and then swallow them whole without them even being aware of it. I knew by its immense size and its lumpy and very bloated body that it had swallowed many victims. And much to my surprise, I could see the victims were still alive inside of it. They were moving inside the creature's ever-stretched belly. I could hear them still carrying on ambitious conversations with others in the lobby.

The serpent's name was "Self-Promotion".

Most of the victims did not know they had been consumed by self-promotion. But some, much to my dismay, had willingly and consciously allowed the snake to engulf them. The goal or intentions of these victims was the same as that of this bloated serpent—they all wanted to become bigger and bigger.

The Charmer: Lust

The second snake that I saw was to my left—a very beautiful-looking creature that almost made me forget the horror of the first. It was a type of chameleon, ever changing colors and appearance according to the desires of those under its power. It could look like whatever you wanted it to: male, female, young, old innocent or seductive. It was swaying back and forth, doing a hypnotic dance. I found myself drawn to it, as were many others.

Suddenly I shuddered with disgust, for I knew this hideous thing. His name was "Lust". I hadn't recognized it at first, for it was incredibly charming.

There was a large group of people gathered all around it, and they were actually flirting and dancing with it and each other. Without even losing the rhythm of its cobra-like movement, Lust would strike its partners with a flash of fangs, with forked tongues that were identical to this serpent's ever flickering tongue; the people spoke deceptive flattery to one another. They were starting to realize that they could use the power for themselves. They could get what they wanted quicker by using the power of Lust. I realized that many of the victims that were now held captive in the belly of Self-Promotion had first been bitten and poisoned by "Lust".

When one is first bitten by Lust, the venom brings a real high. But not for long afterward, its victims become sick. Then often for relief, the victim goes back for another bite (for the venom is very addictive) until he or she is completely consumed with the poison. The victim in turn bites others, and the sickness spreads. I did not look at lust for long, for I knew its enticing power was great and deadly.

Two Snakes: Pride and Insecurity

The next snake I saw was, in fact, two very long snakes. They were intertwined—wrapped all around each other just like snakes do when they are mating. This, by the way is exactly what these were doing. One was red; the other was yellow. They were spinning over and over, making a very uneasy sound that pervaded the whole place. As they twisted and spun around, they appeared to be actually biting each other. All at once I understood that this writhing mass was "Pride" and "Insecurity". They were feeding off each other, and they were reproducing after their own kind.

Then I looked around the room and saw people who were turning yellow and then red. Yellow was the color of Insecurity and red was the color of Pride. People would change into these shades back and forth just like the rotating colors of the spinning serpents.

The whole lobby seemed to be aglow with these colors. The two worked well together, though they seemed to irritate one another. There was a nervous uneasiness building that made me want to scream. These two serpents made those who were affected by them (which were almost everyone, to some extent) feel miserable. However, they didn't want to admit it, because their pride told them that they might look weak, insecure or possibly unsuccessful. So the spinning continued. Pride, Insecurity, Pride Insecurity etc.

Flesh for Scales: The Fear of Man

I was surprised that I even detected what was next. I knew it was only because the Lord was allowing me to see it—I never would have noticed it on my own. I spotted what had first appeared to be someone who had fallen down, but it was much too long to be human. It was hidden half way under the front counter and was entangled among the feet of the people.

The reason I had originally believed it was human was because it appeared to have human skin or flesh. It had what looked like a human head. Though having the color of flesh and having no scales, it was obviously still a snake. It was very low to the ground and earthly.

This one was the "Fear of Man". It didn't have to do very much, because Pride and Insecurity were doing most of its work. It just lay there moving its human-like head back and forth horizontally. Then I noticed that people all across the room were doing the very same thing, almost as if they had been entranced. They were only concerned about who was who, and how they were being perceived by others, so much so that they did not recognize the evil in their midst. This freaky creature blinded its victims from the holy fear of God and injected them with a deadly fear of man instead.

People all across the room were so busy looking at each other that they were unaware that they had become entangled by the fear of man. It would subtly wrap itself around its victims' feet until they could no longer move; they were completely paralyzed with fear. I remembered the scripture: "The fear of man will prove to be a snare," (Proverbs 29:25).

Up High: Jealousy

I then heard a movement above me. I instinctively looked up, and there, much to my distress, I saw another serpent wrapped around the balcony, its endless tail running down the length of the escalator. This one was bright green. It looked like one of those tree snakes—very comfortable with heights. This was "Jealousy" and it was literally green with envy. It was breathing very heavily and seemed to have fire in its eyes. I could tell it was burning up inside. I didn't want it to catch me looking at it, because I was afraid it was ready to explode with fury at any moment.

Jealousy attacked the high places. It couldn't stand to be down low. Its mist-like breath released A FOG OF COMPETITION which filled the room, I could see that those who had breathed in the mist although they were chatting politely with peers, now had that same fire burning down in their eyes as did the serpent. And I knew they would attack and tear down those in the high places in order to obtain these places for themselves. Many of these people had become easy prey for Self-Promotion.

It is amazing how demons hide in our midst and influence us with unbelievable delusions and deceptions.

Unfortunately, many things we ministers do are influenced by the devil. The fighting, the hatred, the self-promotion are not products of the nature of God. They are characteristic of the demonic and a fallen nature.

Chapter 24

Demons and Churches

Please take note of this list of demons commonly found working within the church. It will help you to identify and resist the enemy.

1.	The Spirit of Accusation
2.	Spirit of Gossip
3.	Spirit of Slander
4.	Spirit of Faultfinding
5.	Spirit of Pride
6.	Spirit of Self-Righteousness
7.	Spirit of Respectability
8.	Spirit of Selfish Ambition
9.	Spirit of Unrighteous Judgement
10.	Spirit of Jealousy
11.	Spirit of the Accuser of the Brethren
12.	Spirit of Intimidation
13.	Spirit of Treachery
14.	Spirit of Rejection
15.	Spirit of Bitterness
16.	Spirit of Impatience
17.	Spirit of Unforgiveness
18.	Spirit of Lust
19.	Spirit of Hate
20.	The Spirit of Division

There are many evil spirits in the church and they occupy the minds and hearts of Christians and influence their behaviour. The presence of church splits and infighting is evidence of the work of demons within the Church of Jesus Christ. Another vision related by Rick Joyner clearly illustrates this great truth. It shows how demons use Christians to wreak havoc within the church. Self-righteous and decent looking Christians are frequently used as agents of demons.

As you read this vision, you will recognize many of the principles I have shared in earlier chapters.

- *You will notice how demons operate in groups and teams.*

- *You will also notice how agreement with demons give them power over your life.*

- *You will realize that demons operate against us only through the power of deception.*

Christians are deceived into thinking that their criticisms and judgements are justified. Through this deception, demons wreak havoc in churches all over the world. I have highlighted some important portions so that you do not miss them.

The Vision of Demons in the Church

The demonic army was so large that it stretched as far as I could see. It was separated into divisions, with each carrying a different banner. The foremost divisions marched under the banners of Pride, Self-righteousness, Respectability, Selfish Ambition, Unrighteous Judgement, and Jealousy. There were many more of these evil divisions beyond my scope of vision, but those in the vanguard of this terrible horde from hell seemed to be the most powerful. The leader of this army was the Accuser of the Brethren himself.

The weapons carried by this horde were also named. The swords were named Intimidation; the spears were named Treachery; and the arrows were named Accusation, Gossip,

Slander and Faultfinding. Scouts and smaller companies of demons with such names as Rejection, Bitterness, Impatience, Unforgiveness and Lust were sent in advance of this army to prepare for the main attack.

These smaller companies and scouts were much fewer in number, but they were no less powerful than some of the larger divisions that followed. They were smaller only for strategic reasons. Just as John the Baptist was a single man, but was given an extraordinary anointing for baptizing the masses to prepare them for the Lord, these smaller demonic companies were given extraordinary evil powers for "baptizing the masses." A single demon of Bitterness could sow his poison into multitudes of people, even entire races or cultures. A demon of Lust would attach himself to a single performer, movie, or even advertisement, and send what appeared to be bolts of electric slime that would hit and "desensitise" great masses of people. All of this was to prepare for the great horde of evil, which followed.

This army was marching specifically against the church, but it was attacking everyone that it could. I knew that it was seeking to pre-empt a coming move of God, which was destined to sweep masses of people into the church.

The primary strategy of this army was to cause division on every possible level of relationship - churches with each other, congregations with their pastors, husbands and wives, children and parents, and even children with each other. The scouts were sent to locate the openings in churches, families or individuals that Rejection, Bitterness, Lust, etc., could exploit and make larger. Then the following divisions would pour through the openings to completely overcome their victims.

The most shocking part of this vision was that this horde was not riding on horses, but primarily on Christians! Most of them were well-dressed, respectable, and had the appearance of being refined and educated, but there also seemed to be representatives from almost every walk of life.

These people professed Christian truths in order to appease their consciences, but they lived their lives in agreement with the powers of darkness. As they agreed with those powers their assigned demons grew and more easily directed their actions.

Many of these believers were host to more than one demon, but one would obviously be in charge. The nature of the one in charge dictated which division it was marching in. Even though the divisions were all marching together, it also seemed that at the same time the entire army was on the verge of chaos. For example, the demons of hate, hated the other demons as much as they did the Christians. The demons of jealousy were all jealous of one another. The only way the leaders of this horde kept the demons from fighting each other was to keep their hatred, jealousy, etc., focused on the people they were riding. However, these people would often break out in fights with each other. I knew that this was how some of the armies that had come against Israel in the Scriptures had ended up destroying themselves. When their purpose against Israel was thwarted, their rage was uncontrollable, and they simply began fighting each other.

I noted that the demons were riding on these Christians, but were not in them as was the case with non-Christians. It was obvious that these believers had only to stop agreeing with their demons in order to get free of them.

For example, if the Christian on which a demon of jealousy was riding just started to question the jealousy, that demon would weaken very fast. When this happened the weakening demon would cry out and the leader of the division would direct all of the demons around that Christian to attack him until the bitterness, etc., would build up on him again. If this did not work, the demons would begin quoting Scriptures that were perverted in such a way that would justify the bitterness, accusations, etc.

It was clear that the power of the demons was rooted almost entirely in the power of deception, but they had deceived these Christians to the point where they could use them and they would think they were being used by God.

This was because banners of Self-Righteousness were being carried by almost all of the individuals so that those marching could not even see the banners that marked the true nature of these divisions.

As I looked far to the rear of this army I saw the entourage of the Accuser himself. I began to understand his strategy, and I was amazed that it was so simple.

He knew that a house divided cannot stand, and this army represented an attempt to bring such division to the church that she would completely fall from grace. It was apparent that the only way he could do this was to use Christians to war against their own brethren, and that is why almost everyone in the forward divisions were Christians, or at least professing Christians. Every step that these deceived believers took in obedience to the Accuser strengthened his power over them. This made his confidence and the confidence of all of his commanders grow with the progress of the army as it marched forward. It was apparent that the power of this army depended on the agreement of these Christians with the ways of evil.

Chapter 25

Deliverance Has a Practical Side

**Howbeit Jesus ... saith unto him, Go ...and tell them how
great things the Lord hath done for thee,...**

Mark 5:19

After the Lord has set you free, you need to make practical adjustments, otherwise the demons will return. You need to obey the Word of God practically.

**Then goeth he, and taketh with himself seven other spirits
more wicked than himself, and they enter in and dwell
there: and the last state of that man is worse than the
first...**

Matthew 12:45

Notice from the Scripture that the house was empty, swept and clean. A house, which is not filled with the Word of God, will be filled with demons. I have watched as many go for deliverance sessions and yet never seem to be free. This is because we are ignoring a most basic truth from the Lord.

**And ye shall know the truth, and the truth shall make
you free.**

John 8:32

It is the knowledge of the truth that actually sets us free. Many pastors attempt to use the laying on of hands to accomplish what only the truth can do. However, none of us is wiser than God. We may anoint people with oil a thousand times but that cannot be substituted for the knowledge of truth.

Neither give place to the devil.

Ephesians 4:27

Demons cannot have access to Christians unless we give them a foothold. Demons keep returning because they still have access. Often, the foothold of the devil is not removed and so the demons keep returning. What is there in your life that allows the devil to keep returning? Perhaps bad company is ruining your life. Perhaps, the alcohol you take in is opening the door to the spirit of death. Without some practical steps, your deliverance from demons will never be complete. Jesus told the mad man of Gadara to go around witnessing about what the Lord had done for him. The continued deliverance of this mad man lay in his obedience to this command. What has the Lord asked you to do? Obeying this command will keep you free from demons.

Chapter 26

Be Strong in the Lord

Finally, my brethren, BE STRONG IN THE LORD, and in the power of his might. PUT ON THE WHOLE ARMOUR OF GOD, that ye may be able to stand against the wiles of the devil.

Ephesians 6:10-11

When I was in boarding school, physical strength was an advantage. Form two boys would shout, "One small boy!" and we the junior ones would all have to run.

However, I remember a Form one boy who was bigger and stronger than the rest of us. He decided to ignore the yelling of the Form two boys. They would scream, "One small boy!" but he would totally ignore them. You see, he was bigger and stronger than most of the Form two boys and he could beat them up if he wanted to.

As I watched this older and stronger boy, I received instruction: the stronger you are, the less trouble you will receive from certain people.

This is how I came to understand Ephesians 6:10. I realized that if I were strong in the Lord, many problems would automatically fall away. This is exactly what has happened. The stronger I became spiritually, the more distant certain problems were.

God wants us to be strong in spiritual things. Unfortunately, many are strong in other aspects of life. They are strong in their schoolwork, they are strong in politics, they are strong in sports, but they are not strong in the Lord!

God's Word to us is to be strong. That means we can be strong! He did not say, "Pray for strength," neither did He say, "God will strengthen you." He said, "Be strong in the Lord."

As you increase in the strength of the Lord, many of the demonic attacks in your life will lose the power they have.

Chapter 27

Put on the Whole Armour
of God

Finally, my brethren, BE STRONG IN THE LORD, and in the power of his might. PUT ON THE WHOLE ARMOUR OF GOD, that ye may be able to stand against the wiles of the devil.

Ephesians 6:10-11

Protecting yourself from the attacks of the enemy can be very complicated. After September 11, America realized how vulnerable they were. A myriad of attacks could be launched at America from any angle. This fact also holds true for believers and that is why we need the whole armour of God. Several attacks are planned and launched against the believer from different angles. Except we put on the whole armour, we will not be fully protected from the enemy.

One prayer by a prophet does not exclude you from having to put on your armour. The armour protects you in totality and it is time for Christians to put on the whole armour. The different aspects of the armour will keep you from being invaded by demons. I had an experience years ago that served to eternally stamp this fact in my spirit.

The Demon Possessed Girl

I remember a young girl who was possessed with demons. She would stand up while the fellowship leader was preaching and interrupt the service with long prophecies. She would even command the Catholic priest to stop the administration of communion and she would prophesy and make the entire congregation kneel down and stand up at will.

Many of the leaders were inexperienced, and did not know what to do. So they would stand back as this young lady dominated the whole service. I had been told about this young lady who had been controlling the meetings but had never seen her myself.

One day however, I was in a service in which the demons manifested. This young lady stood up and took over the service with her prophecies just as had been described to me. I got out of my seat, took a couple of brothers with me, and escorted her into the basement of the building. I knew that an evil spirit was controlling this young woman. As soon as we got into the basement, her eyes widened.

She looked straight at me and said, "Don't quench the spirit." I could virtually see the demons dancing in her eyes. This almost unsettled me as I wondered, "Was I quenching the Holy Spirit?"

Then I said, "You foul spirit, in the name of Jesus, I command you to stop your activities and come out of this girl." She immediately went into all sorts of writhing movements. The spirit began to manifest, and spoke to us using the girl's voice. I cannot give all the details of this deliverance episode in this book. However, there was one thing that struck me.

I asked the demon spirit, "How did you come into this lady?"

The spirit said, "The belt of truth was loose." That demon had gained access to this young girl's life because the protective armour of God was deficient.

I cannot tell you exactly how this girl's belt of truth was loosened. What is important is that a deficiency in the armour had opened the door to evil spirits. Our spiritual armour is well described in Ephesians. Put every single piece on, and you will be blessed!

So use every piece of God's armor to resist the enemy whenever he attacks, and when it is all over, you will still be standing up. But to do this, you will need the strong belt of truth and the breastplate of God's approval. Wear shoes that are able to speed you on as you preach the Good News of peace with God. In every battle you will need faith as your shield to stop the fiery arrows aimed at you by Satan. And you will

need the helmet of salvation and the sword of the Spirit-which is the Word of God. Pray all the time. Ask God for anything in line with the Holy Spirit's wishes. Plead with him, reminding him of your needs, and keep praying earnestly for all Christians everywhere.
Ephesians 6:13-18 TLB

Chapter 28

Freedom in Christ

Stand fast therefore in the LIBERTY WHEREWITH CHRIST HATH MADE US FREE, and be not entangled again with the yoke of bondage.

Galatians 5:1

You are free! You are free from the demons of inferiority! You are free from the demons of self-pity!

You are delivered from the control of the demons of jealousy and envy!

Take authority over the spirit of depression!

You are free from the power of lust!

The power of witchcraft is broken!

Bind the demons of discouragement in your life.

You are free from anxiety!

The spirit of fear and restlessness is bound!

You are free indeed!

I see you overcoming the spirit of bitterness and hatred!

You are free from the power and hold of deception!

Every stronghold of satanic intimidation is pulled down!

Amen!